Michael W. Curran
Professor, Corporate Media Productions
Seneca College
School of Communication Arts
70 The Pond Rd. Toronto Ontario M3J 3M6
416-491-5050 ex3583

ALSO BY STEPHEN R. COVEY

The 7 Habits of Highly Effective People
Principle-Centered Leadership
First Things First

Daily Reflections for

HIGHLY EFFECTIVE PEOPLE

STEPHEN R. COVEY

A FIRESIDE BOOK   Published by Simon & Schuster
New York   London   Toronto   Sydney   Tokyo   Singapore

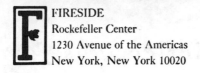

FIRESIDE
Rockefeller Center
1230 Avenue of the Americas
New York, New York 10020

FIRESIDE and colophon are registered trademarks of Simon
& Schuster Inc.

Designed by Crowded House

Manufactured in the United States of America

10 9 8 7 6 5 4 3 2 1

Library of Congress Cataloging-in-Publication Data is available.

ISBN 0-671-88717-3

Foreword

The purpose of this *Reflections* book is to help you become strong in the hard moments. In every day are found a few hard moments, which if we are strong in, make everything else like "a piece of cake." But if we are weak in those moments—if we cave in to the temptation of taking the lower road—then we will find ourselves caving in on many things. As Shakespeare said:

> *There is a tide in the affairs of men,*
> *Which taken at the flood, leads on to fortune;*
> *Omitted, all the voyage of their life*
> *Is bound in shallows and in miseries.*
> *On such a full sea are we now afloat,*
> *And we must take the current when it serves,*
> *Or lose our ventures.*

> *The Tragedy of Julius Caesar,*
> Act 4, Scene 3, Lines 218–224

There are hard moments in each of the 7 Habits. Let me briefly share what some of them might be:

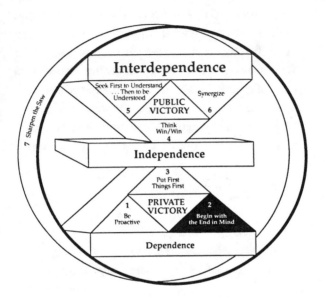

Seven Habits Maturity Continuum

Many of the hard moments of *Habit 1*, "*Be Proactive*," involve subordinating a mood, temporary feeling, or circumstance to a principle or guideline you value. As I related in the *7 Habits* book, one of the most profound, truly inspirational experiences of my life took place in the fall of 1969 when I was on a sabbatical leave in Hawaii to write a book. I was rummaging around the stacks in the library on a campus I had an office in. I pulled down a book which, foolishly, I never recorded. But I remember what it said as distinctly today as the first time I read it. It literally staggered me. I read it again and again that day, and returned several days in a row to reflect on it.

It said essentially this: "Between stimulus and response is a space. In this space lies our freedom to choose our response. In these choices lie our growth and our happiness."

In the most fundamental sense, Habit 1 is the awareness of this space between stimulus and response—between what has happened to us and our response to it. Next to life itself, this self-awareness and our freedom to choose, to direct our lives, is our most precious gift and power.

The hard moment or test of Habit 1 is to be

aware of and to choose to live your own life. It is seeing yourself as the programmer, not as a program being acted out. Regardless of the social and psychic scars you may carry inside, regardless of how others treat you, regardless of the disappointments and strains and setbacks which may blindside your finest intentions, you see the space between all of that and your freedom and power to respond to it.

Habit 2, *"Begin with the End in Mind,"* is the habit of vision, of purpose, of mission. It is a sense of what your life is about and how you want to live it. It includes the principles and guidelines you want to live by. It's also not just your values, for values without vision are insufficient. Yes, we all want to be good, but good for what? We want to be good for something. What is that something? What is that vision— not just for your whole life, but for today, this meeting, this interaction, this hour, this moment?

For many, the test or hard moment for Habit 2

comes when you are tired and lazy—just going with the flow. Some new project or meeting or day begins and you simply do not do the mental, emotional, and spiritual work inside yourself to get a sense of how you would like it to end up. This doesn't mean you decide *all* the exact details of how you want the meeting or day to end up. But rather, you do decide what you want the *spirit* of that day or meeting and the quality of the relationship to end up like. You feel deeply committed to worthy end results and yet no action has been taken.

Habit 3, *"Put First Things First,"* is the habit of integrity, of discipline, of keeping that commitment. It is the habit that draws upon the independent will to literally act upon those things which we, in Habit 2, determined are first things. The hard moments of Habit 3 come at us constantly. Will we carry forth our resolve? Will we execute? The deeper the resolve, the easier the execution—and vice versa.

For instance, perhaps the most powerful form of

minority vocal control ever contemplated takes place when a few million taste buds are screaming "Yes, yes!" to something you shouldn't eat, when at the same time, billions of unvocal cells in the rest of the body are crying out "No, no!" This, frankly, is one of my hardest moments. It usually takes place at the end of the day when I'm on a trip all alone in a hotel room. I'm totally spent and exhausted from speaking all day and then traveling several hundred miles to a new location. I'm relaxed on the bed, talking on the phone to my wife and kids—simply "letting it all hang out." Before the call home I call room service. I can order anything I want. This is a hard moment. When I fail this hard moment, I live with the consequences of not sleeping as deeply, of putting on unnecessary girth, of not having the same energy the next afternoon. I then also have the feeling that I have betrayed my integrity and stewardship to model what I teach and to champion other people's growth around the same principles. True minority control!

*   *   *

What is *your* hardest moment for each of the first three habits? They are usually always different and unique to every person. There is great value in trying to identify them so that you can exercise your unique endowments of self-awareness and independent will to live by your vision and conscience. There is also great value in recognizing the horrendous price we pay, both personally and socially, when we are weak in the hard moments. It's like trading dust for diamonds. Shakespeare beautifully captured the effects of "giving in" to the pleasure of the moment rather than subordinating it to the real joy of contribution and growth:

> *What win I, if I gain the thing I seek?*
> *A dream, a breath, a froth of fleeting joy.*
> *Who buys a minute's mirth to wail a week?*
> *Or seeks eternity to get a toy?*
> *For one sweet grape, who will the vine destroy?*
> *The Rape of Lucrece,*
> Lines 211–215

Perhaps the hardest moment and test of *Habit 4,* *"Think Win-Win,"* is when we are absolutely convinced we are right. We know exactly what should be done, what the decision should be, what we want. It is truly going for win-win when all you really want is your own way—simply winning. Or perhaps it's going for win-win when another takes you on and opposes you, and you are so stirred up that you want to go for win-lose. You see it as a contest of wills; you don't want to give in. Or perhaps the hard moment is when you are threatened by the possibility of displeasing someone and you need their acceptance and approval so badly that you want to go for lose-win. You capitulate and give in, rather than combining courage with consideration.

The hard moment of *Habit 5, "Seek First to Understand, Then to Be Understood,"* comes when you are crying to be understood. Perhaps you feel completely misunderstood. Everyone else is having their say and you are not. Everyone else's feelings and views are being expressed and yours aren't. Besides that, they're off-base and you have a much better idea. You matter, too. They should understand you. You already understand them, but now it's your turn. Besides, understanding them is irrelevant. You know you're right. There's no need to understand that which is wrong—or so you think.

The second hardest moment I face, and the greatest mistakes I make, usually come from violating Habit 5. It's judging before I understand and acting before I really understand either the big picture or another person. Once the collective monologue begins, you start investing more and more of your ego into your convictions and into your own need to be understood. The other just isn't listening. Oh, what a hard moment that is—to reach deep inside and subordinate your need to be understood and really work to get into the frame of mind and heart of the other. It is listening empathically and having the discipline and the patience to simply hold your tongue. It's constantly relearning the anatomy lesson that we have two ears and one mouth, and we should use them accordingly. (Only one of the three holes closes.)

The hard moment or test of *Habit 6*, "*Synergize*," comes when you have a difference with someone and you are tempted to simply compromise. It's taking the course of least resistance by trying to quickly and efficiently find some middle position satisfactory to both, even though you know in your heart it does not optimize the situation. You know there are other unexplored alternatives out there, but there has not yet been enough Habit 5 to really understand the issue and the underlying needs and concerns of the people involved. In short, the temptation is to satisfy rather than to optimize.

The key is to press on with the spirit of Habit 4 and the skill of Habit 5 until the spirit of synergy starts to come into the relationship. Then you are both looking in the same direction and searching for a third alternative whereby you not only tolerate and accept differences, but actually celebrate them. You value the differing perceptions, feelings, and experiences immensely, for they enable you to create something far better. Creating a third alternative that is felt by each person to be superior to those originally proposed becomes one of the most bonding experiences in relationships and in life.

Habit 7, "*Sharpen the Saw*," is essentially the habit that this book represents. It is using our unique gifts and endowments to constantly renew ourselves physically, mentally, and spiritually, and to renew our relationships. In so doing, we counteract entropy—the tendency of all things to eventually break down. One of the most effective ways to renew is through daily reflection and meditation. In both one's heart and mind, the renewal spirit is stirred. The resolve to live by values based on principles is renewed and deepened. Our batteries are recharged. The saw becomes sharper. Your life becomes sharper. You are able to do your work better, faster, wiser. You are better able to love unconditionally, to take initiative, to be both courageous and compassionate simultaneously. You're able to sidestep negative energy rather than give away your "space" to those people or things that seem to control or victimize you. When you don't sidestep, you literally give up your freedom to choose your response. You disempower yourself and empower others' weaknesses to continue to mess up your life. You are not living; you are "being lived."

Habit 7 has many hard moments. For me, the hardest is to simply get up at 5:30 A.M. and climb aboard that stationary bike and start reading when I don't want to—when I'm longing to get back between the sheets, and the siren call of the mattress is ever so seductive. I've also found that the key to my being strong in this hard moment of climbing on that bike is being strong in the hard moment the night before of going to bed at a decent hour.

My next hard moment is paying the price early in the day to develop a frame of mind and heart that's in total alignment with the vision and principles of my personal mission statement—to truly "win" a private victory. I've found that books like *Reflections* can powerfully serve to create that mind and heart. Reflecting is like "priming the pump." The familiar saying goes, "As a man thinketh in his heart, so is he." It takes conscious effort to ponder and meditate—to slow down the rush and the urgency addiction long enough to get perspective and ask, "What's it all about, Alfie?" Putting thoughts from the mind into the heart is the essence of meditation and reflection.

Plato said, "The unexamined life is not worth living," yet keeping a journal so as to observe one's own involvement in life, distilling one's learnings, experiences, feelings, and insights, is a hard moment for many. Turning off the mindless TV viewing and getting back into a challenging, interesting, enlightening, or inspiring book is a hard moment for others.

Reflecting and meditating upon principles of effectiveness which deal with all of life is as vital to our mind and soul as food is to the body. Yesterday's meal will not satisfy today's hunger. Each day we must eat. Each day we must reflect. If "Sharpen the Saw" truly becomes a habit, a deeply ingrained behavior pattern, just as brushing one's teeth or bathing is, and if this habit is done in a balanced, consistent, and wise way, it will affect the quality, productivity, and satisfaction of every other hour of the day. I know of no higher leveraged activity in life that compares with sharpening the saw in all four dimensions—physical, mental, spiritual, and social. Done properly, all the other six habits are exercised, developed, and used. And when we join others in sharpening the saw, relationships are deepened and bonding truly takes place. It moves the fulcrum over and has exponential leverage and synergy.

* * *

When I have media interviews on the *7 Habits*, I am often asked the question, "Do you have any evidence that these are *the* habits of effectiveness? Do you have any empirical proof? Have studies been done?" I used to answer by giving some evidence, quoting studies or sharing anecdotal evidence from people's lives. No longer. All I do now is challenge the interviewer to show me one exception, one truly effective or successful person, family, or organization which violates the principles contained within the habits—effective meaning *both* short- and long-term success, balance, and accomplishment in *all* areas—personal, family, work, etc. They simply can't do it. I would sincerely open this challenge to anyone. Sometimes the interviewers say, "What about this obviously successful person?" I respond, "Now remember how we defined success as long- and short-term balance and accomplishment. How's his relationship with his teenagers?" They often respond, "Well, that's in shambles, but his business is really prospering." "Really," I answer. "Let's look deeper into that business to detect the reasons why it's prospering. Is it possibly because the competitors are dumber or because success in the marketplace is relative? Or is it due to a brilliant market strategy or unique patent position? How long will that last? How strong and healthy is the culture—the goose that lays the golden eggs? Is the trust level high enough to permit people to be empowered so that they can provide consistent quality service to the 'customer' in 'fast, flexible, focused, and friendly ways'?"

The habits are founded on self-evident principles which are almost synonymous with the words, "success" or "effectiveness." True effectiveness is both long- and short-term and balance rather than just the few golden eggs produced in one area of life "today."

On my left shoulder is a small scar. I imagine you have one also—on your shoulder or somewhere else. I remember receiving a smallpox vaccination as a child and getting a bit sick that day. A little smallpox was introduced into my system, but it triggered off an immunity so that I never got a real case of smallpox. You probably haven't, either. I remember that it was a hard moment. It was an unpleasant experience. I feared it. In spite of assurances, I remember the pain. I would have preferred not to have it done. I had no real sense of what it all meant. But my parents insisted and, of course I, like you, am happy we complied. We had to be strong in that hard moment. In considering the possible alternative, the benefits were incalculable.

When we sharpen the saw in a balanced, consistent way, we vaccinate ourselves. Slowly, gradually, even imperceptibly, an immune system develops within so that no matter what problem we face, we are able to tap into our deep inner resources and reserves. It also cultivates the awareness and humility to tap into outer resources when needed. We never really get the disease resulting from unsolved problems because our immune system is sufficiently strong to solve them early on.

This is the reason why AIDS is such a horrific disease. It destroys the very ability to fight disease. It destroys the immune system. People don't die of AIDS; they die of other diseases because they have no immunity to fight against them. Similarly, individuals don't die from setbacks and disappointments; they die from the lack of a "coping" immune system. Marriages don't die from in-law problems or financial challenges; they die from not having an immune system to handle challenges and differences. They "fight or flight" instead of synergistically communicating.

Strong, living immune systems enable us to honestly examine ourselves and our relationships with others. They enable us to make amends, to swallow our pride, and to apologize or make whatever other emotional deposits are necessary to heal, restore, and renew. Each time we do make such deposits, each time we reflect and recommit with real intent, we inoculate ourselves again, and a new immunity is triggered which will enable us to handle even greater setbacks or disappointments that may come our way.

The key to developing a strong immune system in your family is being strong in the hard moment of showing unconditional love to the child that tests you the most—who pushes you to the very limit. When such unconditional love, not permissiveness, is shown to this one, every other child knows that they, too, are unconditionally loved. This knowledge lies at the heart of an intrinsic sense of self-worth and of the abundance mentality. But when love is given conditionally, every other child knows they, too, have to win their love by good behavior, that there is nothing in them of true intrinsic worth. Then they develop their sense of worth and security from a comparison-based identity external to themselves. A scarcity mentality is cultivated, which makes it difficult for them to be genuinely happy for the success of others, including one's own loved ones. They may say they're happy, but inwardly, they're eating their hearts out, and they know it.

Finally, I believe that these seven habits tap into a tremendous reservoir of new capacities and potential that lie within each one of us. However, access to this power is not ultimately found by focusing on self, on turning inward, or on self-improvement. The pattern of true growth and development may occur from the inside-out, but we are driven to it from the outside-in—from the need that all of us have to serve, to matter, to contribute to the lives of others and to society, to be involved in something of transcendent meaning—to leave a legacy. In other words, private victories precede public victories. But unless some meaningful public challenge exists, some need or cause to serve, there will be no private victory, or at best it would only be self-serving. Browning put it succinctly:

There is an answer to the passionate longing of the heart for fullness . . .
Live in all things outside yourself by love, and you will have joy . . .
It is a lesson learned slowly and through difficulty.

Robert Browning, quoted by
David O. McKay in *Cherished Memories*

These habits are foundational; they are generic. The principles are universal. They transcend culture, religion, race, nationality. They are made relevant in situations in the form of practices. Like the blood which flows through the heart into the various parts of the body where it is used in specific ways, so too must principles become practices—specific actions. Every person and his or her situation is unique. Therefore, universal abstract principles must be converted into unique practical actions applicable to that situation. The *hard moments* are in these hard realities of everyday life. I am absolutely convinced that when we are truly strong in the hard moments, everything else is essentially "cake."

The greatest battles of life are fought out every day in the silent chambers of our own heart.

IF WE WANT to change a situation, we first have to change ourselves. And to change ourselves effectively, we first have to change our perceptions.

*p.18**

---

* All page references are to *The 7 Habits of Highly Effective People.*

WE MUST LOOK *at* the lens through which we see the world, as well as at the world we see, and understand that the lens itself shapes how we interpret the world.

p.17

THE *CHARACTER ETHIC*, which I believe to be the foundation of success, teaches that there are basic principles of effective living, and that people can only experience true success and enduring happiness as they learn and integrate these principles into their basic character.

p.18

THE PERSONALITY ETHIC tells me there must be something out there—some new planner or seminar that will help me handle pressures in a more efficient way.

But is there a chance that *efficiency* is not the answer? Is getting more things done in less time going to make a difference—or will it just increase the pace at which I react to the people and circumstances that seem to control my life?

Could there be something I need to see in a deeper, more fundamental way—some paradigm within myself that affects the way I see my time, my life, and my own nature?

p.41

IF I TRY to use human influence strategies and tactics of how to get other people to do what I want, to work better, to be more motivated, to like me and each other—while my character is fundamentally flawed, marked by duplicity and insincerity—then, in the long run, I cannot be successful. My duplicity will breed distrust, and everything I do—even using so-called good human relations techniques—will be perceived as manipulative.

p.21

To FOCUS ON technique is like cramming your way through school. You sometimes get by, perhaps even get good grades, but if you don't pay the price day in and day out, you never achieve true mastery of the subjects you study or develop an educated mind.

p.21–22

WE SIMPLY *ASSUME* that the way we see things is the way they really are or the way they should be. And our attitudes and behaviors grow out of those assumptions.

p.24

EACH OF US has many, many maps in our head, which can be divided into two main categories: maps of the way *things are*, or *realities*, and maps of *the way things should be*, or *values*. We interpret everything we experience through these mental maps.

p.24

MANY PEOPLE EXPERIENCE a fundamental shift in thinking when they face a life-threatening crisis and suddenly see their priorities in a different light, or when they suddenly step into a new role, such as that of husband or wife, parent or grandparent, manager or leader.

p.31

"OBJECTIVE REALITY" IS composed of "light-house" principles that govern human growth and happiness—natural laws that are woven into the fabric of every civilized society throughout history and comprise the roots of every family and institution that has endured and prospered. The degree to which our mental maps accurately describe this territory does not alter its existence.

p.33

PARADIGMS ARE POWERFUL because they create the lens through which we see the world. The power of a paradigm shift is the essential power of quantum change, whether that shift is an instantaneous or a slow and deliberate process.

p.32

WHAT HAPPENS WHEN we attempt to shortcut a natural process in our growth and development? If you are only an average tennis player but decide to play at a higher level in order to make a better impression, what will result? Would positive thinking alone enable you to compete effectively against a professional?

p.36

To RELATE EFFECTIVELY with a wife, a husband, children, friends, or working associates, we must learn to listen. And this requires emotional strength. Listening involves patience, openness, and the desire to understand— highly developed qualities of character. It's so much easier to operate from a low emotional level and to give high-level advice.

p.37

BORROWING STRENGTH BUILDS weakness. It builds weakness in the borrower because it reinforces dependence on external factors to get things done. It builds weakness in the person forced to acquiesce, stunting the development of independent reasoning, growth, and internal discipline. And finally, it builds weakness in the relationship. Fear replaces cooperation, and both people involved become more arbitrary and defensive.

p.39

January 15

As WE LOOK around us and within us and recognize the problems created as we live and interact within the Personality Ethic, we begin to realize that these are deep, fundamental problems that cannot be solved on the superficial level on which they were created.

We need a new level, a deeper level of thinking—a paradigm based on the principles that accurately describe the territory of effective human being and interacting—to solve these deep concerns.

p.42

THE "INSIDE-OUT" APPROACH to personal and interpersonal effectiveness means to start first with self; even more fundamentally, to start with the most *inside* part of self—with your paradigms, your character, and your motives.

The inside-out approach says that private victories precede public victories, that making and keeping promises to ourselves precedes making and keeping promises to others. It says it is futile to put personality ahead of character, to try to improve relationships with others before improving ourselves.

Inside-out is a process—a continuing process of renewal based on the natural laws that govern human growth and progress. It's an upward spiral of growth that leads to progressively higher forms of responsible independence and effective interdependence.

p.43

OUR CHARACTER, BASICALLY, is a composite of our habits. Because they are consistent, often unconscious patterns, they constantly, daily, express our character and produce our effectiveness . . . or ineffectiveness.

p.46

THE SEVEN HABITS are not a set of separate or piecemeal psyche-up formulas. In harmony with the natural laws of growth, they provide an incremental, sequential, highly integrated approach to the development of personal and interpersonal effectiveness. They move us progressively on a Maturity Continuum from *dependence* to *independence* to *interdependence*.

p.48–49

DEPENDENCE IS THE paradigm of you—you take care of me; *you* come through for me; *you* didn't come through; I blame *you* for the results.

Independence is the paradigm of *I*—*I* can do it; *I* am responsible; *I* am self-reliant; *I* can choose.

Interdependence is the paradigm of *we*—*we* can do it; *we* can cooperate; *we* can combine our talents and abilities and create something greater together.

Dependent people need others to get what they want. Independent people can get what they want through their own effort. Interdependent people combine their own efforts with the efforts of others to achieve their greatest success.

p.49

ACHIEVING *UNITY*—ONENESS —with ourselves, with our loved ones, with our friends and working associates, is the highest and best and most delicious fruit of the Seven Habits. Most of us have tasted this fruit of true unity from time to time in the past, as we have also tasted the bitter, lonely fruit of disunity—and we know how precious and fragile unity is.

p.318

PRIVATE VICTORIES PRECEDE *public victories.* You can't invert that process any more than you can harvest a crop before you plant it.

p.51

EFFECTIVENESS LIES IN what I call the P/PC Balance. *P* stands for *production* of desired results, the golden eggs. *PC* stands for *production capability*, the ability or asset that produces the golden eggs, the goose.

p.54

WHEN TWO PEOPLE in a marriage are more concerned about getting the golden eggs, the benefits, than they are in preserving the relationship that makes them possible, they often become insensitive and inconsiderate, neglecting the little kindnesses and courtesies so important to a deep relationship. They begin to use control levers to manipulate each other, to focus on their own needs, to justify their own position and look for evidence to show the wrongness of the other person. The love, the richness, the softness and spontaneity begin to deteriorate. The goose gets sicker day by day.

p.55

YOU CAN BUY people's hands, but you can't buy their hearts. Their hearts are where their enthusiasm, their loyalty is. You can buy their backs, but you can't buy their brains. That's where their creativity is, their ingenuity, their resourcefulness.

p.58

MARILYN FERGUSON OBSERVED, "No one can persuade another to change. Each of us guards a gate of change that can only be opened from the inside. We cannot open the gate of another, either by argument or by emotional appeal."

If you decide to open your "gate of change" to really understand and live the principles embodied in the Seven Habits, your growth will be *evolutionary*, but the net effect will be *revolutionary*.

p.60–61

CHANGE—REAL CHANGE—comes from the inside out. It doesn't come from hacking at the leaves of attitude and behavior with quick fix personality ethic techniques. It comes from striking at the root—the fabric of our thought, the fundamental, essential paradigms, which give definition to our character and create the lens through which we see the world.

p.317

WE ARE NOT our feelings. We are not our moods. We are not even our thoughts. The very fact that we can think about these things separates us from them and from the animal world. Self-awareness enables us to stand apart and examine even the way we "see" ourselves—our self-paradigm, the most fundamental paradigm of effectiveness. It affects not only our attitudes and behaviors, but also how we see other people. It becomes our map of the basic nature of mankind.

p.66–67

You can decide within yourself how circumstances will affect you. Between what happens to you, or the stimulus, and your response to it, is your freedom or power to choose that response.

p.69

THE WORD *PROACTIVE* means more than merely taking initiative. It means that as human beings, we are responsible for our own lives. Our behavior is a function of our decisions, not our conditions. We can subordinate feelings to values. We have the initiative and the responsibility to make things happen.

p.71

THE LAW OF the harvest governs; we will always reap what we sow—no more, no less. The law of justice is immutable, and the closer we align ourselves with correct principles, the better our judgment will be about how the world operates and the more accurate our paradigms—our maps of the territory—will be.

p.305

DON'T ARGUE FOR other people's weaknesses. Don't argue for your own. When you make a mistake, admit it, correct it, and learn from it—immediately.

p.93

PEOPLE WHO EXERCISE their embryonic freedom day after day will, little by little, expand that freedom. People who do not will find that it withers until they are literally "being lived." They are acting out the scripts written by parents, associates, and society.

p.93

February 2

IT'S INCREDIBLY EASY to get caught up in an activity trap, in the busy-ness of life, to work harder and harder at climbing the ladder of success only to discover it's leaning against the wrong wall.

p.98

February 3

WE EACH HAVE a number of different roles in our lives—different areas or capacities in which we have responsibility. I may, for example, have a role as an individual, a husband, a father, a teacher, a church member, and a businessman. And each of these roles is important.*

Writing your mission in terms of the important roles in your life gives you balance and harmony. It keeps each role clearly before you. You can review your roles frequently to make sure that you don't get totally absorbed by one role to the exclusion of others that are equally or even more important in your life.

p.135 and 137

---

* If you would like to see some examples of mission statements, or if you would like a worksheet to help you develop your own, please call 1-800-292-6839. There is no cost to you.

IF WE DO not develop our own self-awareness and become responsible for first creations, we empower other people and circumstances outside our Circle of Influence to shape much of our lives by default.

p.100

AT THE VERY heart of our Circle of Influence is our ability to make and keep commitments and promises. The commitments we make to ourselves and to others, and our integrity to those commitments, is the essence and clearest manifestation of our proactivity.

p.91–92

As a *PRINCIPLE-CENTERED* person, you try to stand apart from the emotion of the situation and from other factors that would act on you, and evaluate the options. Looking at the balanced whole—the work needs, the family needs, other needs that may be involved and the possible implications of the various alternative decisions—you'll try to come up with the best solution, taking all factors into consideration.

p.127

WE ARE LIMITED, but we can push back the borders of our limitations. An understanding of the principle of our own growth enables us to search out correct principles with the confidence that the more we learn, the more clearly we can focus the lens through which we see the world. The principles don't change; our understanding of them does.

p.123

SOMETIMES THERE ARE apparently noble reasons given for making money, such as the desire to take care of one's family. And these things are important. But to focus on money-making as a center will bring about its own undoing.

p.113

PEOPLE CAN'T LIVE with change if there's not a changeless core inside them. The key to the ability to change is a changeless sense of who you are, what you are about and what you value.

p.108

THROUGH IMAGINATION, WE can visualize the uncreated worlds of potential that lie within us. Through conscience, we can come in contact with universal laws or principles with our own singular talents and avenues of contribution, and with the personal guidelines within which we can most effectively develop them. Combined with self-awareness, these two endowments empower us to write our own script.

p.103

TOO OFTEN PARENTS are trapped in the management paradigm, thinking of control, efficiency, and rules instead of direction, purpose, and family feeling.

p.103

IN BUSINESS, THE market is changing so rapidly that many products and services that successfully met consumer tastes and needs a few years ago are obsolete today. Proactive powerful leadership must constantly monitor environmental change, particularly customer buying habits and motives, and provide the force necessary to organize resources in the right direction.

p.102

MANAGEMENT IS CLEARLY different from leadership. Leadership is primarily a high-powered, right brain activity. It's more of an art; it's based on a philosophy. You have to ask the ultimate questions of life when you're dealing with personal leadership issues.

p.147

IF YOU'RE PROACTIVE, you don't have to wait for circumstances or other people to create perspective expanding experiences. You can consciously create your own.

p.131

WHEN PEOPLE SERIOUSLY undertake to identify what really matters most to them in their lives, what they really want to be and to do, they become very reverent. They start to think in larger terms than today and tomorrow.

p.132

ALL THINGS ARE created twice. There's a mental or first creation, and a physical or second creation of all things. You have to make sure that the blueprint, the first creation, is really what you want, that you've thought everything through. Then you put it into bricks and mortar. Each day you go to the construction shed and pull out the blueprint to get marching orders for the day. You begin with the end in mind.

p.99

SOME SITUATIONS ABSOLUTELY require legal process. But I see it as a court of last, not first, resort. If it is used too early, even in a preventive sense, sometimes fear and the legal paradigm create subsequent thought and action processes that are not synergistic.

p.283

YOU CAN'T BECOME principle-centered without first being aware of your paradigms and understanding how to shift them and align them with principles. You can't become principle-centered without a vision of and a focus on the unique contribution that is yours to make.

p.147

YOU HAVE TO decide what your highest priorities are and have the courage—pleasantly, smilingly, nonapologetically—to say "no" to other things. And the way you do that is by having a bigger "yes" burning inside. The enemy of the "best" is often the "good."

p.156–57

February 20

I AM PERSONALLY persuaded that the essence of the best thinking in the area of time management can be captured in a single phrase: *Organize and execute around priorities.*

p.149

EFFECTIVE PEOPLE ARE not problem-minded; they're opportunity-minded. They feed opportunities and starve problems.

p.154

MANY PEOPLE SEEM to think that success in one area can compensate for failure in other areas of life. But can it really? Perhaps it can for a limited time in some areas. But can success in your profession compensate for a broken marriage, ruined health, or weakness in personal character? True effectiveness requires balance.

p.161

YOU CAN'T BE successful with other people if you haven't paid the price of success with yourself.

p.185

HERE ARE TWO ways to put ourselves in control of our lives immediately. We can *make a promise*—and keep it. Or we can *set a goal*—and work to achieve it. As we make and keep commitments, even small commitments, we begin to establish an inner integrity that gives us the awareness of self-control and the courage and strength to accept more of the responsibility for our own lives. By making and keeping promises to ourselves and others, little by little, our honor becomes greater than our moods.

p.92

IF I MAKE deposits into an Emotional Bank Account with you through courtesy, kindness, honesty, and keeping my commitments to you, I build up a reserve. Your trust toward me becomes higher, and I can call upon that trust many times if I need to. I can even make mistakes and that trust level, that emotional reserve, will compensate for it. My communication may not be clear, but you'll get my meaning anyway. You won't make me "an offender for a word." When the trust account is high, communication is easy, instant, and effective.

p.188

CLARIFYING EXPECTATIONS SOMETIMES takes a great deal of courage. It seems easier to act as though differences don't exist and to hope things will work out than it is to face the differences and work together to arrive at a mutually agreeable set of expectations.

p.195

IT TAKES A great deal of character strength to apologize quickly out of one's heart rather than out of pity. A person must possess himself and have a deep sense of security in fundamental principles and values in order to genuinely apologize.

p.197

WHETHER YOU ARE the president of a company or the janitor, the moment you step from independence into interdependence in any capacity, you step into a leadership role. You are in a position of influencing other people. And the habit of effective interpersonal leadership is Think Win/Win.

p.206

MATURITY IS *THE balance between courage and consideration.* If a person can express his feelings and convictions with courage balanced with consideration for the feelings and convictions of another person, he is mature, particularly if the issue is very important to both parties.

p.217

MOST PEOPLE ARE deeply scripted in what I call the Scarcity Mentality. They see life as having only so much, as though there were only one pie out there. And if someone were to get a big piece of the pie, it would mean less for everybody else. The Scarcity Mentality is the zero-sum paradigm of life. That's why a character trait that is essential to Win/Win is the Abundance Mentality, the paradigm that there is plenty out there for everybody.

p.219

So OFTEN THE problem is in the system, not in the people. If you put good people in bad systems, you get bad results. You have to water the flowers you want to grow.

p.232

IF I WERE to summarize in one sentence the single most important principle I have learned in the field of interpersonal relations, it would be this: *Seek first to understand, then to be understood.* This principle is the key to effective interpersonal communication.

p.237

IN EMPHATIC LISTENING, you listen with your eyes and with your heart. You listen for feelings, for meaning. You listen for behavior. You use your right brain as well as your left. You sense, you intuit, you feel. Empathic listening is powerful because it gives you accurate data to work with.

p.241

WIN/WIN AGREEMENTS FOCUS on results, releasing tremendous individual human potential and creating greater synergy, building
Production Capability in the process instead of
focusing exclusively on Production.

p.226

SPEND TIME WITH your children now, one on one. Listen to them; understand them. Look at your home, at school life, at the challenges and the problems they're facing, through their eyes. Build the Emotional Bank Account. Give them psychological air.

p.258

SYNERGY MEANS THAT the whole is greater than the sum of its parts. It means that the relationship the parts have to each other is a part in and of itself. It is not only a part, but the most catalytic, the most empowering, the most unifying, and the most exciting part.

The creative process is also the most terrifying part because you don't know exactly what's going to happen or where it is going to lead. You don't know what new dangers and challenges you'll find. It takes an enormous amount of internal security to begin with the spirit of adventure, discovery, and creativity. Without doubt, you have to leave the comfort zone of base camp and confront an entirely new and unknown wilderness.

p.263

INEFFECTIVE PEOPLE LIVE day after day with unused potential. They experience synergy only in small, peripheral ways in their lives. But creative experiences can be produced regularly, consistently, almost daily in people's lives. It requires enormous personal security and openness and a spirit of adventure.

p.264

THE MORE AUTHENTIC you become, the more genuine in your expression, particularly regarding personal experiences and even self-doubts, the more people can relate to your expression and the safer it makes them feel to express themselves. That expression in turn feeds back on the other person's spirit, and genuine creative empathy takes place, producing new insights and learnings and a sense of excitement and adventure that keeps the process going.

p.267

WHEN A PERSON has access to both the intuitive, creative, and visual right brain and the analytical, logical, verbal left brain, then the whole brain is working. There is psychic synergy taking place in our own head. And this tool is best suited to the reality of what life is, because life is not just logical—it is also emotional.

p.275

KEEPING A JOURNAL of our thoughts, experiences, insights, and learnings promotes mental clarity, exactness, and context. Writing good letters—communicating on the deeper level of thoughts, feelings, and ideas rather than on the shallow, superficial level of events—also affects our ability to think clearly, to reason accurately, and to be understood effectively.

p.296

IT IS EXTREMELY valuable to train the mind to stand apart and examine its own program. That, to me, is the definition of a liberal education—the ability to examine the programs of life against larger questions and purposes and other paradigms. Training, without such education, narrows and closes the mind so that the assumptions underlying the training are never examined. That's why it is so valuable to read broadly and to expose yourself to great minds.

p.295

ECOLOGY IS A WORD that basically describes the synergism in nature—everything is related to everything else. It's in the relationship that creative powers are maximized, just as the real power in these Seven Habits is in their relationship to each other, not just in the individual habits themselves.

p.283

"THE MAP IS not the territory." A map is simply an explanation of certain aspects of the territory. While individuals may look at their own lives and interactions in terms of paradigms or maps emerging out of their experience and conditioning, these maps are not the territory. They are a "subjective reality," only an attempt to describe the territory.

p.23 and 33

THE WAY WE see the problem *is* the problem.

p.40

IT BECOMES OBVIOUS that if we want to make relatively minor changes in our lives, we can perhaps appropriately focus on our attitudes and behaviors. But if we want to make significant, quantum change, we need to work on our basic paradigms.

p.31

THE CHARACTER ETHIC is based on the fundamental idea that there are *principles* that govern human effectiveness—natural laws in the human dimension that are just as real, just as unchanging and unarguably "there" as laws such as gravity are in the physical dimension.

p.32

THE GLITTER OF the Personality Ethic is that there is some quick and easy way to achieve quality of life—personal effectiveness and rich, deep relationships with other people—without going through the natural process of work and growth that makes it possible.

It's symbol without substance. It's the "get rich quick" scheme promising "wealth without work." And it might even appear to succeed— but the schemer remains.

And trying to get high quality results with its techniques and quick fixes is just about as effective as trying to get to someplace in Chicago using a map of Detroit.

p.35–36

ON A TEN-POINT scale, if I am at level two in any field, and desire to move to level five, I must first take the step toward level three.* "A thousand-mile journey begins with the first step" and can only be taken one step at a time.

p.37

* If you would like to receive a complimentary self-scoring Seven Habits Personal Feedback Profile to help you evaluate your current level of effectiveness, please call 1-800-292-6839.

PRINCIPLES ARE LIKE lighthouses. They are natural laws that cannot be broken. As Cecil B. De Mille observed of the principles contained in his monumental movie *The Ten Commandments*, "It is impossible for us to break the law. We can only break ourselves against the law."

p.33

EFFECTIVE INTERDEPENDENCE CAN only be built on a foundation of true independence.

p.185

REALLY HELPING OUR children grow may involve being patient enough to allow them the sense of possession as well as being wise enough to teach them the value of giving, and providing the example ourselves.

p.40

LOVE IS SOMETHING you do: the giving of self, the sacrifices you make, even for people who offend or do not love in return. Love is a value that is actualized through loving actions.

p.80

ALBERT EINSTEIN OBSERVED, "The significant problems we face cannot be solved at the same level of thinking we were at when we created them."

p.42

THE INSIDE-OUT APPROACH says if you want to *have* a happy marriage, *be* the kind of person who generates positive energy and sidesteps negative energy rather than empowering it. If you want to *have* a more pleasant, cooperative teenager, *be* a more understanding, empathic, consistent, loving parent. If you want to *have* more freedom, more latitude in your job, *be* a more responsible, a more helpful, a more contributing employee. If you want to be trusted, *be* trustworthy. If you want the secondary greatness of recognized talent, focus first on the primary greatness of character.

p.43

THE GRAVITY PULL of some of our habits may currently be keeping us from going where we want to go. But it is also gravity pull that keeps our world together, that keeps the planets in their orbits and our universe in order. It is a powerful force, and if we use it effectively, we can use the gravity pull of habit to create the cohesiveness and order necessary to establish effectiveness in our lives.

p.47

By WORKING ON knowledge, skill, and desire, we can break through to new levels of personal and interpersonal effectiveness as we break with old paradigms that may have been a source of pseudo-security for years.

p.47

HAPPINESS CAN BE defined, in part at least, as the fruit of the desire and ability to sacrifice what we want *now* for what we want *eventually*.

p.48

MUCH OF OUR current emphasis on independence is a reaction to dependence—to having others control us, define us, use us, and manipulate us.

The little understood concept of interdependence appears to many to smack of dependence, and therefore, we find people, often for selfish reasons, leaving their marriages, abandoning their children, and forsaking all kinds of social responsibility—all in the name of independence.

p.50

THE SEVEN HABITS are habits of *effectiveness*. Because they are based on principles, they bring the maximum long-term beneficial results possible. They become the basis of a person's character, creating an empowering center of correct maps from which an individual can effectively solve problems, maximize opportunities, and continually learn and integrate other principles in an upward spiral of growth.

p.52

PC (PRODUCTION CAPABILITY) work is treating employees as volunteers just as you treat customers as volunteers, because that's what they are. They volunteer the best part—their hearts and minds.

p.58

April 1

As YOU OPENLY, honestly share what you're learning with others, you may be surprised to find that negative labels or perceptions others may have of you tend to disappear. Those you teach will see you as a changing, growing person, and will be more inclined to be helpful and supportive as you work, perhaps together, to integrate the Seven Habits into your lives.

p.60

April 2

UNTIL WE TAKE how we see ourselves (and how we see others) into account, we will be unable to understand how others see and feel about themselves and their world. Unaware, we will project our intentions on their behavior and call ourselves objective.

p.67

BE PATIENT WITH yourself. Self-growth is tender; it's holy ground. There's no greater investment.

p.62–63

BETWEEN STIMULUS AND *response, one has the freedom to choose.* Within the freedom to choose are those endowments that make us uniquely human: *self-awareness; imagination* (the ability to create in our minds beyond our present reality); *conscience* (a deep inner awareness of the principles that govern our behavior, and a sense of the degree to which our thoughts and actions are in harmony with them); and *independent will* (the ability to act based on our self-awareness, free of all other influences.)

p.70

April 5

HIGHLY PROACTIVE PEOPLE recognize their "response-ability"—the ability to chose their response. They do not blame circumstances, conditions, or conditioning for their behavior. Their behavior is a product of their own conscious choice, based on values, rather than a product of their conditions, based on feeling.

p.71

REACTIVE PEOPLE FOCUS on circumstances over which they have no control. The negative energy generated by that focus, combined with neglect in areas they could do something about, causes their Circle of Influence to shrink. Proactive people focus their efforts on the things they can do something about. The nature of their energy is positive, enlarging, and magnifying, causing their Circle of Influence to increase.

p.83

April 7

THE POWER TO MAKE and keep commitments to ourselves is the essence of developing the basic habits of effectiveness.

p.92

April 8

LOOK AT THE weaknesses of others with compassion, not accusation. It's not what they're not doing or should be doing that's the issue. The issue is your own chosen response to the situation and what you should be doing. If you start to think the problem is "out there," stop yourself. That thought is the problem.

p.93

THE PROBLEMS WE face fall in one of three areas: direct control (problems involving our own behavior); indirect control (problems involving other people's behavior); or no control (problems we can do nothing about, such as our past or situational realities). Changing our habits, changing our methods of influence and changing the way we see our no control problems are all within our Circle of Influence. So whether a problem is direct, indirect, or no control, we have in our hands the first step to the solution.

p.85–86

HOW DIFFERENT OUR lives are when we really know what is deeply important to us, and keeping that picture in mind, we manage ourselves each day to be and to do what really matters most.

p.98

IN DEVELOPING OUR own self-awareness many of us discover ineffective scripts, deeply embedded habits that are totally unworthy of us, totally incongruent with the things we really value in life. We are response-able to use our imagination and creativity to write new ones that are more effective, more congruent with our deepest values and with the correct principles that gives our values meaning.

p.104

April 12

DID YOU EVER consider how ridiculous it would be to try to cram on a farm—to forget to plant in spring, play all summer, and then cram in the fall to bring in the harvest? The farm is a natural system. The price must be paid and the process followed. You always reap what you sow; there is no shortcut.

p.22

IF MY SENSE of security lies in my reputation or in the things I have, my life will be in a constant state of threat and jeopardy that these possessions may be lost or stolen or devalued. If I'm in the presence of someone of greater net worth or fame or status, I feel inferior. If I'm in the presence of someone of lesser net worth or fame or status, I feel superior. My sense of self-worth constantly fluctuates. I don't have any sense of constancy or anchorage or persistent selfhood. I am constantly trying to protect and insure my assets, properties, securities, position, or reputation.

p.114

WHEN YOU ARE coming from a principle-centered paradigm, you are not being acted upon by other people or circumstances. You are proactively choosing what you determine to be the best alternative. You make your decision consciously and knowledgeably.

p.127

TO SEEK SOME abstract meaning to our lives out in our Circle of Concern is to abdicate our proactive responsibility, to place our own first creation in the hands of circumstance and other people.

p.128

PERSONAL LEADERSHIP IS not a singular experience. It is, rather, the ongoing process of keeping your vision and values before you and aligning your life to be congruent with those most important things. And in that effort, your powerful right brain capacity can be a great help to you on a daily basis as you work to integrate your personal mission statement into your life. It's another application of "begin with the end in mind."

p.132

THE MOST EFFECTIVE way I know to begin with the end in mind is to develop a *personal mission statement* or philosophy or creed. It focuses on what you want to be (character) and to do (contributions and achievements) and on the values or principles upon which being and doing are based.

Because each individual is unique, a personal mission statement will reflect that uniqueness, both in content and form.

p.106

KEEP IN MIND that you are always saying "no" to something. If it isn't to the apparent, urgent things in your life, it is probably to the more fundamental; highly important things. Even when the urgent is good, the good can keep you from your best, keep you from your unique contribution, if you let it.

p.157

"TIME MANAGEMENT" IS really a misnomer—the challenge is not to manage time, but to manage ourselves.

p.150

April 20

IF YOU ARE an effective manager of your self, your discipline comes from within; it is a function of your independent will. You are a disciple, a follower, of your own deep values and their source. And you have the will, the integrity, to subordinate your feelings, your impulses, your moods to those values.

p.148

April 21

YOU SIMPLY CAN'T think *efficiency* with people. You think *effectiveness* with *people* and *efficiency* with *things*. I've tried to be "efficient" with a disagreeing or disagreeable person and it simply doesn't work. I've tried to give ten minutes of "quality time" to a child or an employee to solve a problem, only to discover such "efficiency" creates new problems and seldom resolves the deepest concern.

p.169–70

April 22

INTERDEPENDENCE IS A choice only independent people can make. Unless we are willing to achieve real independence, it's foolish to try to develop human relations skills. We might even have some degree of success when the sun is shining. But when the difficult times come— and they will—we won't have the foundation to keep things together.

p.186–87

YOU CAN'T TALK your way out of problems you behave yourself into.

p.186

OUR MOST CONSTANT relationships, like marriage, require our most constant deposits into the Emotional Bank Account. With continuing expectations, old deposits evaporate. If you suddenly run into an old high school friend you haven't seen for years, you can pick up right where you left off because the earlier deposits are still there. But your accounts with the people you interact with on a regular basis require more constant investment.

p.189

INTEGRITY MEANS AVOIDING any communication that is deceptive, full of guile, or beneath the dignity of people. "A lie is any communication with intent to deceive." Whether we communicate with words or behavior, if we have integrity, our intent cannot be to deceive.

p.197

WIN/WIN IS A frame of mind and heart that constantly seeks mutual benefit in all human interactions. Win/Win means that agreements or solutions are mutually beneficial, mutually satisfying. With a Win/Win solution, all parties feel good about the decision and feel committed to the action plan. Win/Win sees life as a cooperative, not a competitive arena.

p.207

IF YOU WANT to interact effectively with me, to influence me—your spouse, your child, your neighbor, your boss, your coworker, your friend—you first need to understand me. And you can't do that with technique alone. If I sense you're using some technique, I sense duplicity, manipulation. I wonder why you're doing it, what your motives are. And I don't feel safe enough to open myself up to you.

p.238

EMPATHIC LISTENING GETS inside another person's frame of reference. You look out through it, you see the world the way they see the world, you understand their paradigm, you understand how they feel.

Empathy is not sympathy. Sympathy is a form of agreement, a form of judgment. And it is sometimes the more appropriate emotion and response, but people often feed on sympathy. It makes them dependent. The essence of empathic listening is not that you agree with someone; it's that you fully, deeply, understand that person, emotionally as well as intellectually.

p.240

WHEN WE REALLY, deeply understand each other, we open the door to creative solutions and third alternatives. Our differences are no longer stumbling blocks to communication and progress. Instead, they become the stepping-stones to synergy.

p.259

NEXT TIME YOU catch yourself inappropriately using one of the autobiographical responses—probing, evaluating, advising, or interpreting—try to turn the situation into a deposit by acknowledgement and apology. (*"I'm sorry, I just realized I'm not really trying to understand. Could we start again?"*)

p.260

MOST ALL CREATIVE endeavors are somewhat unpredictable. They often seem ambiguous, hit-or-miss, trial and error. And unless people have a high tolerance for ambiguity and get their security from integrity to principles and inner values, they find it unnerving and unpleasant to be involved in highly creative enterprises. Their need for structure, certainty, and predictability is too high.

p.264–65

How MUCH NEGATIVE energy is typically expended when people try to solve problems or make decisions in an interdependent reality? How much time is spent in confessing other people's sins, politicking, rivalry, interpersonal conflict, protecting one's backside, masterminding, and second guessing? It's like trying to drive down the road with one foot on the gas and the other foot on the brake!

p.274

THE ESSENCE OF synergy is to value differences—to respect them, to build on strengths, to compensate for weaknesses.

p.263

THE MORE GENUINE the involvement, the more sincere and sustained the participation in analyzing and solving problems, the greater the release of everyone's creativity and of their commitment to what they create. This, I'm convinced, is the essence of power in the Japanese approach to business, which has changed the world marketplace.

p.283

WITHOUT INVOLVEMENT, THERE is no commitment. Mark it down, asterisk it, circle it, underline it.

No involvement, no commitment.

p.143

WHEN WE TAKE time to draw on the leadership center of our lives, what life is ultimately all about, it spreads like an umbrella over everything else. It renews us, it refreshes us, particularly if we recommit to it.

p.294

AT SOME TIME in your life, you probably had someone believe in you when you didn't believe in yourself. They scripted you. Did that make a difference in your life?

What if you were a positive scripter, an affirmer, of other people?

p.300

EACH OF US tends to think we see things as they are, that we are *objective*. But this is not the case. We see the world, not as *it is*, but as *we* are—or, as we are conditioned to see it.

p.28

THE MORE CLOSELY our maps or paradigms are aligned with principles or natural laws, the more accurate and functional they will be. Correct maps will infinitely impact our personal and interpersonal effectiveness far more than any amount of effort expended on changing our attitudes and behaviors.

p.35

I BELIEVE THAT we are embryonic and can develop and release more and more potential, develop more and more talents. Highly related to this principle of *potential* is the principle of *growth*—the process of releasing potential and developing talents, with the accompanying need for principles such as *patience, nurturance,* and *encouragement*.

p.34

May 11

IF YOU DON'T let a teacher know at what level you are—by asking a question, or revealing your ignorance—you will not learn or grow. You cannot pretend for long, for you will eventually be found out. Admission of ignorance is often the first step in our education. Thoreau taught, "How can we remember our ignorance, which our growth requires, when we are using our knowledge all the time?"

p.37

Is IT POSSIBLE that my spouse isn't the real problem? Could I be empowering my spouse's weaknesses and making my life a function of the way I'm treated? Do I have some basic paradigm about my spouse, about marriage, about what love really is, that is feeding the problem?

p.42

KNOWING I NEED to listen and knowing how to listen is not enough. Unless I *want* to listen, unless I have the desire, it won't be a habit in my life.

p.47

I SUGGEST THAT you shift the paradigm of your own involvement in this material from the role of learner to that of teacher. Take an inside-out approach, and read with the purpose in mind of sharing or discussing what you learn with someone else within forty-eight hours after you learn it. You will not only better remember what you read, but your perspective will be expanded, your understanding deepened, and your motivation to apply the material increased.

p.60

THE KIND OF reaction that results in people "throwing off their shackles," becoming "liberated," "asserting themselves," and "doing their own thing" often reveals more fundamental dependencies that cannot be run away from because they are internal rather than external—dependencies such as letting the weaknesses of other people ruin our emotional lives or feeling victimized by people and events out of our control.

p.50

IF YOU ADOPT a pattern of life that focuses on golden eggs and neglects the goose, you will soon be without the asset that produces golden eggs. On the other hand, if you only take care of the goose with no aim toward the golden eggs, you soon won't have the wherewithal to feed yourself or the goose.

p.54

ALWAYS TREAT YOUR *employees exactly as you want them to treat your best customers.*

p.58

WHAT DO WE reflect to others about themselves? And how much does that reflection influence their lives? We have so much we can invest in the Emotional Bank Accounts of other people. The more we can see people in terms of their unseen potential, the more we can use our imagination rather than our memory, with our spouse, our children, our coworkers or employees.

p.301

As YOU LIVE your values, your sense of identity, integrity, control, and inner-directedness will infuse you with both exhilaration and peace. You will define yourself from within, rather than by people's opinions or by comparisons to others.

Ironically, you'll find that as you care less about what others think of you, you will care more about what others think of themselves and their worlds, including their relationship with you. You'll no longer build your emotional life on other people's weaknesses. In addition, you'll find it easier and more desirable to change because there is something—some core deep within—that is essentially changeless.

p.61

OUR UNIQUE HUMAN endowments lift us above the animal world. The extent to which we exercise and develop these endowments empowers us to fulfill our uniquely human potential.

p.70

May 21

BETWEEN STIMULUS AND response is our greatest power—the freedom to choose.

p.70

BECAUSE WE ARE, by nature, proactive, if our lives are a function of conditioning and conditions, it is because we have, by conscious decision or by default, chosen to empower those things to control us.

p.71

OUR LANGUAGE IS a very real indicator of the degree to which we see ourselves as proactive people. The language of reactive people absolves them of responsibility.

"That's me. That's just the way I am." *I am determined. There's nothing I can do about it.*

"I can't do that. I just don't have the time." *Something outside me—limited time—is controlling me.*

"If only my wife were more patient." *Someone else's behavior is limiting my effectiveness.*

"I have to do it." *Circumstances or other people are forcing me to do what I do. I'm not free to choose my own actions.*

That language comes from a basic paradigm of determinism. And the whole spirit of it is the transfer of responsibility. *I am not responsible, not able to choose my response.*

p.78

A SERIOUS PROBLEM with reactive language is that it becomes a self-fulfilling prophecy. People become reinforced in the paradigm that they are determined, and they produce evidence to support the belief. They feel increasingly victimized and out of control, not in charge of their life or their destiny. They blame outside forces—other people, circumstances, even the stars—for their own situation.

p.79

IT IS IN the ordinary events of every day that we develop the proactive capacity to handle the extraordinary pressures of life. It's how we make and keep commitments, how we handle a traffic jam, how we respond to an irate customer or a disobedient child. It's how we view our problems and where we focus our energies.

p.92

DIRECT CONTROL PROBLEMS (those involving our own behavior) are solved by working on our habits.

Indirect control problems (those involving other people's behavior) are solved by changing our methods of influence. I have personally identified over thirty separate methods of human influence—as separate as empathy is from confrontation, or example from persuasion. Most people have only three or four of these methods in their repertoire, starting usually with reasoning, and, if that doesn't work, moving on to flight or fight. How liberating it is to accept the idea that I can learn new methods of human influence instead of constantly trying to use old ineffective methods to "shape up" someone else!

p.86

NO CONTROL PROBLEMS (those we can do nothing about) involve taking the responsibility to change the line on the bottom of our face—to smile, to genuinely and peacefully accept these problems and learn to live with them, even though we don't like them. In this way, we do not empower these problems to control us. We share in the spirit embodied in the Alcoholics Anonymous prayer, "Lord, give me the courage to change the things I can, the serenity to accept the things I cannot, and the wisdom to know the difference."

p.86

IF THE LADDER is not leaning against the right wall, every step we take just gets us to the wrong place faster.

p.98

PROBABLY THE MOST important deposit you can make into an Emotional Bank Account is just to listen, without judging or preaching or reading your own autobiography into what someone says. Just listen and seek to understand. Let him feel your concern for him, your acceptance of him as a person.

He may not respond at first. But as those genuine deposits keep coming, they begin to add up. That overdrawn balance is shrinking.

p.190

"IF YOU'RE GOING to bow, bow low," says Eastern wisdom. "Pay the uttermost farthing," says the Christian ethic. To be a deposit, an apology must be sincere. And it must be perceived as sincere.

Leo Roskin taught, "It is the weak who are cruel. Gentleness can only be expected from the strong."

p.198

MANY EXECUTIVES, MANAGERS, and parents swing back and forth, as if on a pendulum, from Win/Lose inconsideration to Lose/Win indulgence. When they can't stand confusion and lack of structure, direction, expectation, and discipline any longer, they swing back to Win/Lose—until guilt undermines their resolve and drives them back to Win/Lose again.

p.210

IT IS POSSIBLE to be busy—very busy—without being very effective.

p.98

WHETHER WE ARE aware of it or not, whether we are in control of it or not, there is a first creation to every part of our lives. We are either the second creation of our own proactive design, or we are the second creation of other people's agendas, of circumstances, or of past habits.

p.100

I CAN CHANGE. I can live out of my imagination instead of my memory. I can tie myself to my limitless potential instead of my limiting past. I can become my own first creator.

p.105

ONCE YOU HAVE a sense of mission, you have the essence of your own proactivity. You have the vision and the values that direct your life. You have the basic direction from which you set your long- and short-term goals. You have the power of a written constitution based on correct principles, against which every decision concerning the most effective use of your time, your talents, and your energies can be effectively measured.

p.108–9

PRINCIPLES ALWAYS HAVE natural consequences attached to them. There are positive consequence when we live in harmony with the principles. There are negative consequences when we ignore them. But because these principles apply to everyone, whether or not they are aware, this limitation is universal. And the more we know of correct principles, the greater is our personal freedom to act wisely.

p.123

EXPAND YOUR PERSPECTIVE by expanding your mind. Visualize in rich detail. Involve as many emotions and feelings as possible. Involve as many of the senses as you can.

p.131

AN EFFECTIVE GOAL focuses primarily on results rather than activity. It identifies where you want to be, and, in the process, helps you determine where you are. It gives you important information on how to get there, and it tells you when you have arrived. It unifies your efforts and energy. It gives meaning and purpose to all you do.

p.137

MY OWN MAXIM of personal effectiveness is this: *Manage from the left* (brain); *lead from the right* (brain).

p.147

June 9

ONLY WHEN YOU have the self-awareness to examine your program—and the imagination and conscience to create a new, unique, principle-centered program to which you can say "yes"—only then will you have sufficient independent will power to say "no," with a genuine smile, to the unimportant.

p.158

RATHER THAN FOCUSING on *things* and *time*, focus on preserving and enhancing *relationships* and on accomplishing *results*.

p.150

WE ACCOMPLISH ALL that we do through delegation—either to time or to other people. If we
delegate to time, we think *efficiency*. If we delegate to other people, we think *effectiveness*.

p.171

REAL SELF-RESPECT COMES from dominion over self, from true independence.

p.186

YOU CAN'T HAVE the fruits without the roots. It's the principle of sequencing: Private Victory precedes Public Victory. Self-mastery and self-discipline are the foundation of good relationships with others.

p.186

IF YOU CULTIVATE the habit of always keeping the promises you make, you build bridges of trust that span the gaps of understanding between you and others.

p.194

INTEGRITY INCLUDES BUT goes beyond honesty. Honesty is telling the truth—in other words, *conforming our words to reality*. Integrity is *conforming reality to our words*—in other words, keeping promises and fulfilling expectations. This requires an integrated character, a oneness, primarily with self but also with life.

p.195–96

DAG HAMMARSKJÖLD, PAST Secretary-General of the United Nations, once made a profound, far-reaching statement: "It is more noble to give yourself completely to one individual than to labor diligently for the salvation of the masses."

p.201

CERTAINLY THERE IS a place for Win/Lose thinking in truly competitive and low-trust situations. But most of life is not a competition. We don't have to live each day competing with our spouse, our children, our coworkers, our neighbors, and our friends. "Who's winning in your marriage?" is a ridiculous question. If both people aren't winning, both are losing.

p.208–9

THE ABUNDANCE MENTALITY flows out of a deep inner sense of personal worth and security. It is the paradigm that there is plenty out there and enough to spare for everybody. It results in sharing of prestige, of recognition, of profits, of decision making. It opens possibilities, options, alternatives, and creativity.

p.219–20

June 19

UNLESS I OPEN up with you, unless you understand me and my unique situation and feelings, you won't know how to advise or counsel me. What you say is good and fine, but it doesn't quite pertain to me.

p.238

June 20

You will never be able to truly step inside
another person, to see the world as he sees it,
until you develop the pure desire, the strength
of personal character, and the positive Emotional Bank Account, as well as the empathic
listening skills to do it.

p.248

WHILE PRACTICES ARE situationally specific, principles are deep, fundamental truths that have universal application. They apply to individuals, to marriages, to families, to private and public organizations of every kind. When these truths are internalized into habits, they empower people to create a wise variety of practices to deal with different situations.

p.35

Go out with your spouse on a regular basis. Have dinner or do something together you both enjoy. Listen to each other; seek to understand. See life through each other's eyes.

p.258

SYNERGY IS EVERYWHERE in nature. If you plant two plants close together, the roots commingle and improve the quality of the soil so that both plants will grow better than if they were separated. If you put two pieces of wood together, they will hold much more than the total of the weight held by each separately. The whole is greater than the sum of its parts. One plus one equals three or more.

p.263

June 24

LIKE THE FAR Eastern philosophy, "We seek not to imitate the masters, rather we seek what they sought," we seek not to imitate past creative synergistic experiences; rather we seek new ones around new and different and sometimes higher purposes.

p.269

June 25

YOU CAN BE synergistic within yourself even in the midst of a very adversarial environment. You don't have to take insults personally. You can sidestep negative energy; you can look for the good in others and utilize that good, as different as it may be, to improve your point of view, and to enlarge your perspective.

p.283–84

MOST OF US think we don't have enough time to exercise. What a distorted paradigm! We don't have time not to. We're talking about three to six hours a week—or a minimum of thirty minutes a day, every other day. That hardly seems an inordinate amount of time considering the tremendous benefits in terms of the impact on the other 162–165 hours of the week.

p.289

EDUCATION—CONTINUALLY HONING and expanding the mind—is vital mental renewal. Sometimes that involves the external discipline of the classroom or systematized study programs; more often it does not. Proactive people can figure out many, many ways to educate themselves.

p.295

MOVING ALONG THE upward spiral requires us to *learn*, *commit*, and *do* on increasingly higher planes. We deceive ourselves if we think that any one of these is sufficient. To keep progressing, we must learn, commit, and do—learn, commit, and do—and learn, commit, and do again.

p.306

THE MORE AWARE we are of our basic paradigms, maps, or assumptions, and the extent
to which we have been influenced by our experience, the more we can take responsibility
for those paradigms, examine them, test them
against reality, listen to others and be open to
their perceptions, thereby getting a larger picture and a far more objective view.

p.29

THE CONSEQUENCES OF attempting to shortcut the natural process of growth in the business world can be dire. Executives may attempt to "buy" a new culture of improved productivity, quality, morale, and customer service with strong speeches, smile training, and external interventions, or through mergers, acquisitions, and friendly or unfriendly takeovers. But they ignore the low-trust climate produced by such manipulations. When these methods don't work, they look for other Personality Ethic techniques that will—all the time ignoring and violating the natural principles and processes on which a high-trust culture is based.

p.38

July 1

IF YOU REALLY seek to understand, without hypocrisy and without guile, there will be times when you will be literally stunned with the pure knowledge and understanding that will flow to you from another human being. It isn't even always necessary to talk in order to empathize. In fact, sometimes words may just get in your way. That's one very important reason why technique alone will not work. That kind of understanding transcends technique.

p.252

THERE ARE TIMES to teach and times not to teach. When relationships are strained and the air charged with emotion, an attempt to teach is often perceived as a form of judgment and rejection. But to take your child alone, quietly, when the relationship is good and to discuss the teaching or the value seems to have much greater impact.

p.40

TRUE INDEPENDENCE OF character empowers us to act rather than be acted upon. It frees us from our dependence on circumstances and other people and is a worthy, liberating goal. But it is not the ultimate goal in effective living.

p.50

July 4

HAVE YOU EVER invaded principal to increase your standard of living, to get more golden eggs? The decreasing principal has decreasing power to produce interest or income. And the dwindling capital becomes smaller and smaller until it no longer supplies even basic needs.

p.55

July 5

YOU ARE NOT your habits. You can replace old patterns of self-defeating behavior with new patterns, new habits of effectiveness, happiness, and trust-based relationships. I encourage you to open the gate of change and growth.

p.61

THE ABILITY TO subordinate an impulse to a value is the essence of the proactive person. Reactive people are driven by feelings, by circumstances, by conditions, by their environment. Proactive people are driven by values—carefully though about, selected, and internalized values.

p.72

ONE WAY TO determine which circle our concern is in, and therefore how proactive we are, is to distinguish between the *have's* and the *be's*. The Circle of Concern (those things that concern us but over which we have no real control) is filled with the *have's*:

"I'll be happy *when I have* my house paid off."

"*If only I had* a boss who wasn't such a dictator . . ."

"*If only I had* a more patient husband . . ."

"*If I had* more obedient kids . . ."

"*If I had* my degree . . ."

"*If I could just have* more time to myself . . ."

The Circle of Influence (those things that we can do something about) is filled with the *be's*—I can *be* more patient, *be* wise, *be* loving. It's the character focus.

p.89

UNTIL A PERSON can say deeply and honestly, "I am what I am today because of the choices I made yesterday," that person cannot say, "I choose otherwise."

p.72

LOVE—THE FEELING—is a fruit of love, the verb.

Reactive people make it a feeling. Hollywood has generally scripted us to believe that we are not responsible, that we are a product of our feelings. But the Hollywood script does not describe the reality. If our feelings control our actions, it is because we have abdicated our responsibility and empowered them to do so.

p.80

LOSE/WIN PEOPLE BURY a lot of feelings. And unexpressed feelings come forth later in uglier ways. Psychosomatic illnesses often are the re-incarnation of cumulative resentment, deep disappointment and disillusionment repressed by the Lose/Win mentality. Disproportionate rage or anger, overreaction to minor provoca-tion, and cynicism are other embodiments of suppressed emotion.

People who are constantly repressing, not transcending feelings toward a higher meaning find that it affects the quality of their self-esteem and eventually the quality of their re-lationships with others.

p.209

July 11

REALLY SEEKING TO understand another person is probably one of the most important Emotional Bank Account deposits you can make, and it is the key to every other deposit. What is important to the other person must be as important to you as the other person is to you.

p.190–91

IMPORTANCE HAS TO do with results. If something is important, it contributes to your mission, your values, your high priority goals. But if we don't have a clear idea of what is important, of the results we desire in our lives, we are easily diverted into responding to the urgent.

p.151

July 13

BEGIN TODAY WITH the image, picture, or paradigm of the end of your life as your frame of reference or the criterion by which everything else is examined. By keeping that end clearly in mind, you can make certain that whatever you do on any particular day does not violate the criteria you have defined as supremely important, and that each day of your life contributes in a meaningful way to the vision you have of your life as a whole.

p.98

MANAGEMENT IS A bottom line focus: How can I best accomplish certain things? Leadership deals with the top line: What are the things I want to accomplish? Management is efficiency in climbing the ladder of success; leadership determines whether the ladder is leaning against the right wall.

p.101

July 15

WHEN YOU CAN see only two alternatives—yours and the "wrong" one—you can look for a synergistic third alternative. There's almost always a third alternative, and if you work with a Win/Win philosophy and really seek to understand, you usually can find a solution that will be better for everyone concerned.

p.284

July 16

AN ORGANIZATIONAL MISSION statement—one that truly reflects the deep shared vision and values of everyone within that organization— creates a great unity and tremendous commitment. It creates in people's hearts and minds a frame of reference, a set of criteria or guidelines, by which they will govern themselves. They don't need someone else directing, controlling, criticizing, or taking cheap shots. They have bought into the changeless core of what the organization is about.

p.143

WHATEVER IS AT the center of our life will be the source of our security, guidance, wisdom, and power.

p.109

As a PRINCIPLE-CENTERED person, you see things differently. And because you see things differently, you think differently, you act differently. Because you have a high degree of security, guidance, wisdom, and power that flows from a solid, unchanging core, you have the foundation of a highly proactive and highly effective life.

p.128

ALMOST ALL OF the world-class athletes and other peak performers are visualizers. They see it; they feel it; they experience it before they actually do it. They begin with the end in mind.

You can do it in every area of your life. Before a performance, a sales presentation, a difficult confrontation, or the daily challenge of meeting a goal, see it clearly, vividly, relentlessly, over and over again. Create an internal "comfort zone." Then, when you get into the situation, it isn't foreign. It doesn't scare you.

p.134

THE CORE OF any family is what is changeless, what is always going to be there—shared vision and values. By writing a family mission statement, you give expression to its true foundation.

p.138

IN ADDITION TO self-awareness, imagination, and conscience, it is the fourth human endowment—*independent will*—that really makes effective self-management possible. It is the ability to make decisions and choices and to act in accordance with them. It is the ability to act rather than to be acted upon, to proactively carry out the program we have developed through the other three endowments. Empowerment comes from learning how to use this great endowment in the decisions we make every day.

p.147–48

IN THE WORDS of the architectural maxim, *form follows function*. Likewise, management follows leadership. The way you spend your time is a result of the way you see your time and the way you really see your priorities.

p.158

WHILE YOU CAN think in terms of *efficiency* in dealing with time, a principle-centered person thinks in terms of *effectiveness* in dealing with people. There are times when principle-centered living requires the subordination of schedules to people.

p.161

July 24

MOST PEOPLE SAY their main fault is a lack of discipline. On deeper thought, I believe that the basic problem is that their priorities have not become deeply planted in their hearts and minds. They attempt to give priority to important but not urgent activities and integrate them into their lives through self-discipline alone. But without a principle center and a personal mission statement they don't have the necessary foundation to sustain their efforts. They're working on the leaves, on the attitudes and the behaviors of discipline, without even thinking to examine the roots, the basic paradigms from which their natural attitudes and behaviors flow.

p.157–58

July 25

IT IS IMPOSSIBLE to achieve Public Victory with popular "Win/Win negotiation" techniques or "reflective listening" techniques or "creative problem-solving" techniques that focus on personality and truncate the vital character base. Effective interdependence can only be achieved by truly independent people.

p.203

THE MOST IMPORTANT ingredient we put into any relationship is not what we say or what we do, but what we are. And if our words and our actions come from superficial human relations techniques (the Personality Ethic) rather than from our own inner core (the Character Ethic), others will sense that duplicity. We simply won't be able to create and sustain the foundation necessary for effective interdependence.

p.187

OUR TENDENCY IS to project out of our own autobiographies what we think other people want or need. We project our intentions on the behavior of others. If they don't interpret our effort as a deposit, our tendency is to take it as a rejection of our well-intentioned effort and to give up.

p.192

INTEGRITY IN AN interdependent reality is simply this: you treat everyone by the same set of principles. As you do, people will come to trust you. They may not at first appreciate the honest confrontational experiences such integrity might generate. Confrontation takes considerable courage, and many people would prefer to take the course of least resistance, belittling and criticizing, betraying confidences, or participating in gossip about others behind their backs. But in the long run, people will trust and respect you if you are honest and open and kind with them. You care enough to confront. And to be trusted, it is said, is greater than to be loved. In the long run, I am convinced, to be trusted will be also to be loved.

p.196–97

MANY OF THE problems in organizations stem from relationship difficulties at the very top. It truly takes more nobility of character to confront and resolve those issues than it does to continue to diligently work for the many projects and people "out there."

p.201

WHEN PARENTS SEE their children's problems as opportunities to build the relationship instead of as negative, burdensome irritations, it totally changes the nature of parent-child interaction. Parents become more willing, even excited, about deeply understanding and helping their children. When a child comes to them with a problem, instead of thinking, "Oh, no! Not another problem!" their paradigm is, "Here is a great opportunity for me to really help my child and to invest in our relationship." Many interactions change from transactional to transformational, and strong bonds of love and trust are created as children sense the value parents give to their problems and to them as individuals.

p.203

WIN/WIN IS A belief in the Third Alternative. It's not your way or my way; it's a *better* way, a higher way.

p.207

PUBLIC VICTORY DOES not mean victory over other people. It means success in effective interaction that brings mutually beneficial results to everyone involved. Public Victory means working together, communicating together, making things happen together that even the same people couldn't make happen by working independently. Public Victory is an outgrowth of the Abundance Mentality paradigm.

p.220

IT IS MUCH more ennobling to the human spirit to let people judge themselves than to judge them. And in a high trust culture, it's much more accurate. In many cases people know in their hearts how things are going much better than the records show. Discernment is often far more accurate than either observation or measurement.

p.224

UNLESS YOU'RE INFLUENCED by my uniqueness, I'm not going to be influenced by your advice. So if you want to be really effective in the habit of interpersonal communication, you cannot do it with technique alone. You have to build the skills of empathic listening on a base of character that inspires openness and trust. And you have to build the Emotional Bank Accounts that create a commerce between hearts.

p.239

August 4

ALL THE WELL-MEANING advice in the world won't amount to a hill of beans if we're not addressing the real problem. And we'll never get to the problem if we're so caught up in our own autobiography, our own paradigm, that we don't take off our glasses long enough to see the world from another point of view.

p.250

August 5

OFTEN WHEN PEOPLE are really given the chance to open up, they unravel their own problems and the solutions become clear to them in the process.

p.251–52

COULD SYNERGY NOT create a new script for the next generation—one that is more geared to service and contribution, and is less protective, less adversarial, less selfish; one that is more open, more trusting, more giving, and is less defensive, protective, and political; one that is more loving, more caring, and is less possessive and judgmental?

p.263

THE PERSON WHO is truly effective has the humility and reverence to recognize his own perceptual limitations and to appreciate the rich resources available through interaction with the hearts and minds of other human beings.

p.277

THE GOLDEN RULE says to "Do unto others as you would have others do unto you." While on the surface that could mean to do for them what you would like to have done for you, I think the more essential meaning is to understand them deeply as individuals, the way you would want to be understood, and then to treat them in terms of that understanding.

p.192

THE DEGREE TO which we have developed our independent will in our everyday lives is measured by our personal integrity. Integrity is, fundamentally, the value we place on ourselves. It's our ability to make and keep commitments to ourselves, to "walk our talk." It's honor with self, a fundamental part of the Character Ethic, the essence of proactive growth.

p.148

THE SUCCESSFUL PERSON has the habit of doing the things failures don't like to do. They don't like doing them either necessarily. But their disliking is subordinated to the strength of their purpose.

That subordination requires a purpose, mission, a clear sense of direction and value, a burning "yes!" inside that makes it possible to say "no" to other things. It also requires independent will, the power to do something when you don't want to do it, to be a function of your values rather than a function of the impulse or desire of any given moment. It's the power to act with integrity to your proactive first creation.

p.148–49

THE KEY IS not to prioritize what's on your schedule, but to schedule your priorities. And this can best be done in the context of the week.

p.161

IDEALLY, THERE IS harmony, unity, and integrity between your vision and mission, your roles and goals, your priorities and plans, and your desires and discipline. In your weekly planner, there should be a place for your personal mission statement so that you can constantly refer to it. There also needs to be a place for your roles and for both short- and long-term goals.

p.160–61

YOUR ECONOMIC SECURITY does not lie in your job; it lies in your own power to produce—to think, to learn, to create, to adapt. That's true financial independence.

p.304

August 14

INTRINSIC SECURITY COMES from service, from helping other people in a meaningful way. One important source is your work, when you see yourself in a contributive and creative mode, really making a difference. Another source is anonymous service—no one knows it and no one necessarily ever will. And that's not the concern; the concern is blessing the lives of other people. Influence, not recognition, becomes the motive.

p.298–99

August 15

OUR PARADIGMS ARE the source of our attitudes and behaviors. We cannot act with integrity outside of them. We simply cannot maintain wholeness if we talk and walk differently than we see.

p.28

IN THE SHORT run, in an artificial social system such as school, you may be able to get by if you learn how to manipulate the man-made rules, to "play the game." In most one-shot or short-lived human interactions, you can use the Personality Ethic to get by and to make favorable impressions through charm and skill and pretending to be interested in other people's hobbies. But eventually, if there isn't deep integrity and fundamental character strength, the challenges of life will cause true motives to surface and human relationship failure will replace short-term success.

p.22

PRINCIPLES ARE NOT *values*. A gang of thieves can share values, but they are in violation of the fundamental principles we're talking about. Principles are the territory. Values are maps. When we value correct principles, we have truth—a knowledge of things as they are

p.35

SOMETIMES WE GET social mileage out of our children's good behavior, and in our eyes, some children simply don't measure up. Our *image* of ourselves, and our role as good, caring parents can be even deeper than our *image* of our children and perhaps influence it. There can be a lot more wrapped up in *the way we see* and handle problems than our concern for our children's welfare. It is then that, instead of trying to change them, we should try to stand apart—to separate *us* from *them*—and to sense their identity, individuality, separateness, and worth.

p.19–20

August 19

As WE CONTINUE to grow and mature, we become increasingly aware that all of nature is *interdependent*, that there is an ecological system that governs nature, including society. We further discover that the higher reaches of our nature have to do with our relationships with others—that human life also is interdependent.

p.49

WHEN PEOPLE FAIL to respect the Production/ Production Capability Balance in their use of physical assets in organizations, they decrease organizational effectiveness and often leave others with dying geese.

p.57

IF THE ONLY vision we have of ourselves comes from the social mirror—from the current social paradigm and from the opinions, perceptions, and paradigms of the people around us—our view of ourselves is like the reflection in the crazy mirror room at the carnival.

p.67

MANY PEOPLE WAIT for something to happen or someone to take care of them. But people who end up with the good jobs are the proactive ones who are solutions to problems, not problems themselves, who seize the initiative to do whatever is necessary, consistent with correct principles, to get the job done.

p.75

Do we have the power to choose our responses?

As a woman in one of my audiences shared, "When I finally realized that I do have that power, when I swallowed that bitter pill and realized that I had chosen to be miserable, I also realized that I could choose not to be miserable."

p.73

WHEN TWO WIN/LOSE people get together—
that is, when two determined, stubborn, ego-
invested individuals interact—the result will
be Lose/Lose. Both will lose. Both will become vindictive and want to "get back" or "get
even," blind to the fact that murder is suicide,
that revenge is a two-edged sword.

p.210

THE REAL KEY to your influence with me is your example, your actual conduct. Your example flows naturally out of your character, or the kind of person your truly are—not what others say you are or what you may want me to think you are. It is evident in how I actually experience you.

Your character is constantly radiating, communicating. From it, in the long run, I come to instinctively trust or distrust you and your efforts with me.

p.238

KEEPING A COMMITMENT or a promise is a major deposit into the Emotional Bank Account; breaking one is a major withdrawal.

p.193

VALUING THE DIFFERENCES is the essence of synergy—the mental, the emotional, the psychological differences between people. And the key to valuing those differences is to realize that all people see the world, not as it is, but as they are.

p.277

BY CENTERING OUR lives on timeless, unchanging principles, we create a fundamental paradigm of effective living. It is the center that puts all other centers in perspective.

p.123

THE EXTENT TO which you begin with the end in mind often determines whether or not you are able to create a successful enterprise. Most business failures begin in the first creation, with problems such as undercapitalization, misunderstanding of the market, or lack of a business plan.

p.99

WE ARE MORE in need of a vision or destination and a compass (a set of principles or directions) and less in need of a road map. We often don't know what the terrain ahead will be like or what we will need to go through it; much will depend on our judgment at the time. But an inner compass will always give us direction.

p.101

SECURITY AND CLEAR guidance bring true wisdom, and wisdom becomes the spark or catalyst to release and direct power. When these four factors are present together, harmonized and enlivened by each other, they create the great force of a noble personality, a balanced character, a beautifully integrated individual.

p.110

September 1

IN EFFECTIVE PERSONAL leadership, visualiza-
tion and affirmation techniques emerge naturally out of a foundation of well thought
through purposes and principles that become
the center of a person's life. They are extremely powerful in rescripting and repro-
gramming, into writing deeply committed-to
purposes and principles into one's heart and
mind.

p.134–35

As WELL AS empowering you to put first things first, weekly organizing* gives you the freedom and the flexibility to handle unanticipated events, to shift appointments if you need to, to savor relationships and interactions with others, to deeply enjoy spontaneous experiences, knowing that you have proactively organized your week to accomplish key goals in every area of your life.

p.165

* If you would like a free one-month supply of weekly worksheets from The Seven Habits Organizer, please call 1-800-292-6839.

TAKING A FEW minutes each morning to review your schedule can put you in touch with the value-based decisions you made as you organized the week as well as unanticipated factors that may have come up. As you overview the day, you can see that your roles and goals provide a natural prioritization that grows out of your innate sense of balance. It is a softer, more right-brain prioritization that ultimately comes out of your sense of personal mission.

p.165

THE CAUSE OF almost all relationship difficulties is rooted in conflicting or ambiguous expectations around roles and goals. Whether we are dealing with the question of who does what at work, how you communicate with your daughter when you tell her to clean her room, or who feeds the fish and takes out the garbage, we can be certain that unclear expectations will lead to misunderstanding, disappointment, and withdrawals of trust.

p.194–95

MANY PEOPLE REFUSE to delegate to other people because they feel it takes too much time
and effort and they could do the job better
themselves. But effectively delegating to others is perhaps the single most powerful high-
leverage activity there is.

p.171

September 6

I HAVE FOUND that the key to the ninety-nine is the one—particularly the one that is testing the patience and the good humor of the many. It is the love and the discipline of the one student, the one child, that communicates love for the others. It's how you treat the one that reveals how you regard the ninety-nine, because everyone is ultimately a one.

p.197

CREATING THE UNITY necessary to run an effective business or a family or a marriage requires great personal strength and courage. No amount of technical administrative skill in laboring for the masses can make up for lack of nobility of personal character in developing relationships. It is at a very essential, one-on-one level that we live the primary laws of love and life.

p.202

ANYTHING LESS THAN Win/Win in an interdependent reality is a poor second best that will have impact in the long-term relationship. The cost of that impact needs to be carefully considered. If you can't reach a true Win/Win, you're very often better off to go for No Deal.

p.214

No deal basically means that if we can't find a solution that would benefit us both, we agree to disagree agreeably—No Deal. No expectations have been created, no performance contracts established. I don't hire you or we don't take on a particular assignment together because it's obvious that our values or our goals are going in opposite directions. It is so much better to realize this up front instead of downstream when expectations have been created and both parties have been disillusioned.

When you have No Deal as an option in your mind, you feel liberated because you have no need to manipulate people, to push your own agenda, to drive for what you want. You can be open. You can really try to understand the deeper issues underlying the positions.

p.213

EFFECTIVE INTERPERSONAL LEADERSHIP requires the vision, the proactive initiative, and the security, guidance, wisdom, and power that come from principle-centered personal leadership.

p.216

"SEEK FIRST TO understand" involves a very deep shift in paradigm. We typically seek first to be understood. Most people do not listen with the intent to understand; they listen with the intent to reply. They're either speaking or preparing to speak. They're filtering everything through their own paradigms, reading their autobiography into other people's lives.

If they have a problem with someone—a son, a daughter, a spouse, an employee—their attitude is, "That person just doesn't understand."

p.239

EMPATHIC LISTENING IS deeply therapeutic and healing because it gives a person "psychological air."

If all the air were suddenly sucked out of the room you're in right now, you wouldn't care about this book; you wouldn't care about anything except getting air. Survival would be your only motivation.

But now that you have air, it doesn't motivate you. *Satisfied needs do not motivate.* It's only the unsatisfied need that motivates. Next to physical survival, the greatest need of a human being is psychological survival—to be understood, to be affirmed, to be validated, to be appreciated.

p.241

WHEN YOU CAN present your own ideas clearly, specifically, visually, and most important, contextually—in the context of a deep understanding of another's paradigms and concerns—you significantly increase the credibility of your ideas.

p.257

IF TWO PEOPLE have the same opinion, one is unnecessary. It's not going to do me any good at all to communicate with someone else who sees the same thing. I don't want to talk, to communicate, with someone who agrees with me; I want to communicate with you because you see it differently. I value that difference.

So when I become aware of the difference in our perceptions, I say, "Good! You see it differently! Help me see what you see."

p.278

WHEN YOU COMMUNICATE synergistically, you are simply opening your mind and heart and expressions to new possibilities, new alternatives, new options. It may seem as if you are casting aside Habit 2 (to begin with the end in mind); but, in fact, you're doing the opposite—you're fulfilling it. You're not sure when you engage in synergistic communication how things will work out or what the end will look like, but you do have an inward sense of excitement and security and adventure, believing that it will be significantly better than it was before. And that is the end that you have in mind.

p.264

MANY PEOPLE THINK if you're nice, you're not tough. But Win/Win is nice . . . and tough. It's twice as tough as Win/Lose. To go for Win/Win, you not only have to be nice, you have to be courageous. You not only have to be empathic, you have to be confident. You not only have to be considerate and sensitive, you have to be brave. To do that, to achieve that balance between courage and consideration, is the essence of real maturity and is fundamental to Win/Win.

p.217–18

ONCE WE ARE self-aware, we must choose purposes and principles to live by; otherwise the
vacuum will be filled, and we will lose our
self-awareness and become like groveling ani-
mals who live primarily for survival and prop-
agation.

p.305

To TRY TO change outward attitudes and behaviors does very little good in the long run if
we fail to examine the basic paradigms from
which those attitudes and behaviors flow.

p.28

PRINCIPLES ARE GUIDELINES for human conduct that are proven to have enduring, permanent value. They're fundamental. They're essentially unarguable because they are self-evident. One way to quickly grasp the self-evident nature of principles is to simply consider the absurdity of attempting to live an effective life based on their opposites. I doubt that anyone would seriously consider unfairness, deceit, baseness, uselessness, mediocrity, or degeneration to be a solid foundation for lasting happiness and success.

p.35

IN THE LAST analysis, what we *are* communicates far more eloquently than anything we *say* or *do*.

p.22

THE MORE PEOPLE are into quick fix and focus on the acute problems and pain, the more that very approach contributes to the underlying chronic condition.

p.40

September 22

LIFE IS, BY nature, highly interdependent. To try to achieve maximum effectiveness through independence is like trying to play tennis with a golf club—the tool is not suited to the reality.

Interdependence is a far more mature, more advanced concept. If I am physically interdependent, I am self-reliant and capable, but I also realize that you and I working together can accomplish far more than, even at my best, I could accomplish alone. If I am emotionally interdependent, I derive a great sense of worth within myself, but I also recognize the need for love, for giving, and for receiving love from others. If I am intellectually interdependent, I realize that I need the best thinking of other people to join with my own.

p.51

EXCESSIVE FOCUS ON P (production) results in ruined health, worn-out machines, depleted bank accounts, and broken relationships. Too much focus on PC (production capability) is like a person who runs three or four hours a day, bragging about the extra ten years of life it creates, unaware he's spending them running. Or a person endlessly going to school, never producing, living on other people's golden eggs—the eternal student syndrome.

p.59

IT'S NOT WHAT happens to us, but our response to what happens to us that hurts us. Of course, things can hurt us physically or economically and can cause sorrow. But our character, our basic identity, does not have to be hurt at all. In fact, our most difficult experiences become the crucibles that forge our character and develop the internal powers, the freedom to handle difficult circumstances in the future and to inspire others to do so as well.

p.73

PROACTIVE PEOPLE CAN carry their own weather with them. Whether it rains or shines makes no difference to them. They are value driven; and if their value is to produce good quality work, it isn't a function of whether the weather is conducive to it or not.

p.71–72

IT'S THE NATURE of reactive people to absolve themselves of responsibility. It's so much safer to say, "I am not responsible." If I say "I am responsible," I might have to say, "I am irresponsible." It would be very hard for me to say that I have the power to choose my response and that the response I have chosen has resulted in my involvement in a negative, collusive environment, especially if for years I have absolved myself of responsibility for results in the name of someone else's weaknesses.

p.88

THE UNIQUE HUMAN capacities of self-awareness, imagination, and conscience enable us to examine first creations and make it possible for us to take charge of our own first creation, to write our own script.

p.100

A TENDENCY THAT'S run through your family for generations can stop with you. You're a transition person—a link between the past and the future. And your own change can affect many, many lives downstream.

You can write it in your personal mission statement and into your mind and heart. You can visualize yourself living in harmony with that mission statement in your Daily Private Victory. You can take steps to love and forgive your own parents, and if they are still living, to build a positive relationship with them by seeking to understand.

p.316

THE LEADER IS the one who climbs the tallest tree, surveys the entire situation, and yells, "Wrong jungle!"

But how do the busy, efficient producers and managers often respond? "Shut up! We're making progress!"

p.101

As YOU AUTHENTICALLY seek to understand, as you rephrase content and reflect feeling, you give a person psychological air. You also help him work through his own thoughts and feelings. As he grows in his confidence of your sincere desire to really listen and understand, the barrier between what's going on inside him and what's actually being communicated to you disappears. It opens a soul-to-soul flow. He's not thinking and feeling one thing and communicating another. He begins to trust you with his innermost tender feelings and thoughts.

p.249

EFFECTIVENESS—OFTEN EVEN survival—does not depend solely on how much effort we expend, but on whether or not the effort we expend is in the right jungle.

p.101

As WE GO deeply within ourselves, as we understand and realign our basic paradigms to bring them in harmony with correct principles, we create both an effective, empowering center and a clear lens through which we can see the world. We can then focus that lens on how we, as unique individuals, relate to that world.

p.128

THE IMAGINATION CAN be used to achieve the fleeting success that comes when a person is focused on material gain or on "what's in it for me." But I believe the higher use of imagination is in harmony with the use of conscience to transcend self and create a life of contribution based on unique purpose and on the principles that govern interdependent reality.

p.135

HAVING SEEN THE power of principle-centered organizing transform the lives of hundreds of people, I am persuaded it makes a difference—a quantum positive difference. And the more completely weekly goals are tied into a wider framework of correct principles and into a personal mission statement, the greater the increase in effectiveness will be.

p.168

STEWARDSHIP DELEGATION IS focused on results instead of methods. It gives people a choice of method and makes them responsible for results. Stewardship delegation involves clear, up-front mutual understanding and commitment regarding expectations. It takes more time in the beginning, but it's time well invested because you can increase your leverage.

p.173–74

PEOPLE ARE VERY TENDER, very sensitive inside. I don't believe age or experience makes much difference. Inside, even within the most toughened and callous exteriors, are the tender feelings and emotions of the heart. That's why in relationships, the little things are the big things.

p.193, 192

ONE OF THE most important ways to manifest integrity is to *be loyal to those who are not present.* In doing so, we build the trust of those who are present. When you defend those who are absent, you retain the trust of those present.

p.196

THERE'S NO WAY to go for a Win in our own lives if we don't even know, in a deep sense, what constitutes a Win—what is, in fact, harmonious with our innermost values. And if we can't make and keep commitments to ourselves as well as to others, our commitments become meaningless. We know it; others know it. They sense duplicity and become guarded. There's no foundation of trust and Win/Win becomes an ineffective superficial technique. Integrity is the cornerstone in the foundation.

p.217

IT IS ONE thing to make a mistake, and quite another thing not to admit it. People will forgive mistakes, because mistakes are usually of the mind, mistakes of judgment. But people will not easily forgive the mistakes of the heart, the ill intention, the bad motives, the prideful justifying cover-up of the first mistake.

p.199

YOU MAY BE scripted in the abundance mentality; I may be scripted in the scarcity mentality. You may approach problems from a highly visual, intuitive, holistic right brain paradigm; I may be very left brain, very sequential, analytical, and verbal in my approach.

Our perceptions can be vastly different. And yet we both have lived with our paradigms for years, thinking they are "facts," and questioning the character or the mental competence of anyone who can't "see the facts."

Now, with all our differences, we're trying to work together—in a marriage, in a job, in a community service project. So how do we transcend the limits of our individual perceptions and come up with Win/Win solutions?

The answer is seek first to understand, then to be understood.

p.253–54

Is IT LOGICAL that two people can disagree and that both can be right? It's not logical: it's *psychological*. And it's very real.

p.277

Synergy means that $1 + 1$ may equal 8, 16, or even 1,600. The synergistic position of high trust produces solutions better than any originally proposed, and all parties know it. Furthermore, they genuinely enjoy the creative enterprise. A miniculture is formed to satisfy in and of itself. Even if it is short-lived, the Production/Production Capability balance is there.

p.271

EACH OF US has roots and the ability to trace those roots, to identify our ancestors.

The highest and most powerful motivation in doing that is not for ourselves only, but for our *posterity*, for the posterity of all mankind. As someone once observed, "There are only two lasting bequests we can give our children—one is roots, the other wings."

p.316

IN THE WORDS of Thoreau, "For every thousand hacking at the leaves of evil, there is one striking at the root." We can only achieve quantum improvements in our lives as we quit hacking at the leaves of attitude and behavior and get to work on the root, the paradigms from which our attitudes and behaviors flow.

p.31

DIFFICULT CIRCUMSTANCES OFTEN create paradigm shifts, whole new frames of reference by which people see the world and themselves and others in it, and what life is asking of them. This new, larger perspective reflects the attitudinal values that lift and inspire us all.

p.75

INTERDEPENDENCE IS A choice only independent people can make. Dependent people cannot choose to become interdependent. They don't have the character to do it; they don't own enough of themselves.

p.51

To MAINTAIN THE Production/Production Capability balance, the balance between the golden egg (production) and the health and welfare of the goose (production capability) is often a difficult judgment call. But I suggest it is the very essence of effectiveness.

p.59

THERE ARE THREE central values in life—the experiential, or that which happens to us; the creative, or that which we bring into existence; and the attitudinal, or our response in difficult circumstances. The highest of these is attitudinal. In other words, what matters most is how we *respond* to what we experience in life.

p.74–75

IT IS so much easier to blame other people, conditioning, or conditions for our own stagnant situation. But we are responsible—"response-able"—to control our lives and to powerfully influence our circumstances by working on *be*, on what we are.

p.89

ACT OR BE acted upon.

p.76

October 21

EFFECTIVE MANAGEMENT IS *putting first things first*. While leadership decides what "first things" are, it is management that puts them first, day-by-day, moment-by-moment. Management is discipline, carrying it out.

p.148

To BEGIN WITH the end in mind means to begin each day with my deepest values firmly in mind. Then as the vicissitudes, as the challenges come, I can make my decisions based on those values. I can act with integrity. I don't have to react to the emotion, the circumstance. I can be truly proactive, value driven, because my values are clear.

p.105–106

As YOU GO through your week, there will un-
doubtedly be times when your integrity will
be placed on the line. The popularity of reacting to the urgent but unimportant priorities of
other people or the pleasure of escaping to unimportant and not urgent activities will
threaten to overpower the important activities
you have planned. Your principle center, your
self-awareness, and your conscience can provide a high degree of intrinsic security, guidance, and wisdom to empower you to use your
independent will and maintain integrity to the
truly important.

p.169

HOLDING PEOPLE TO the responsible course is not demeaning; it is affirming. Proactivity is part of human nature, and, although the pro-active muscles may be dormant, they are there. By respecting the proactive nature of other people, we provide them with at least one clear, undistorted reflection from the social mirror.

p.76

As ONE SUCCESSFUL parent said about raising children, "Treat them all the same by treating them differently," respecting their differences.

p.192

THE STRONGER YOU are—the more genuine your character, the higher your level of proactivity, the more committed you really are to Win/Win—the more powerful your influence will be with another person. This is the real test of interpersonal leadership. It goes beyond *transactional* leadership into *transformational* leadership, transforming the individuals involved as well as the relationship.

p.222

EMPATHIC LISTENING IS risky. It takes a great deal of security to go into a deep listening experience because you open yourself up to be influenced. You become vulnerable. It's a paradox, in a sense, because in order to have influence, you have to be influenced. That means you have to really understand.

p.243

WHEN PROPERLY UNDERSTOOD, synergy is the highest activity in all life. Synergy is the essence of principle-centered leadership. It is the essence of principle-centered parenting. It catalyzes, unifies, and unleashes the greatest powers within people.

p.262

THERE IS TRANSCENDENT power in a strong intergenerational family. An effectively interdependent family of children, parents, grandparents, aunts, uncles, and cousins can be a powerful force in helping people have a sense of who they are and where they came from and what they stand for.

p.315

I DO NOT agree with the popular success literature that says self-esteem is primarily a matter of mind-set, of attitude—that you can psyche yourself into peace of mind.

Peace of mind comes when your life is in harmony with true principles and values and in no other way.

p.298

WHETHER THEY SHIFT us in positive or negative directions, whether they are instantaneous or developmental, paradigm shifts move us from one way of seeing the world to another. And those shifts create powerful change. Our paradigms, correct or incorrect, are the sources of our attitudes and behaviors, and ultimately our relationships with others.

p.30

IT IS NOT what others do or even our own mistakes that hurt us the most; it is our response to those things. Chasing after the poisonous snake that bites us will only drive the poison through our entire system. It is far better to take measures immediately to get the poison out.

p.91

BUSINESSES, COMMUNITY GROUPS, organizations of every kind—including families—can be proactive. They can combine the creativity and resourcefulness of proactive individuals to create a proactive culture within the organization. The organization does not have to be at the mercy of the environment; it can take the initiative to accomplish the shared values and purposes of the individuals involved.

p.77

WHEN YOU'RE DEALING with a person who is coming from a paradigm of Win/Lose, the relationship is still the key. The place to focus is on your Circle of Influence. You make deposits into the Emotional Bank Account through genuine courtesy, respect, and appreciation for that person and for the other point of view. You stay longer in the communication process. You listen more, you listen in greater depth. You express yourself with greater courage. You aren't reactive. You go deeper inside yourself for strength of character to be proactive. You keep hammering it out until the other person begins to realize that you genuinely want the resolution to be a real win for both of you. That very process is a tremendous deposit in the Emotional Bank Account.

p.221

A PERSONAL MISSION statement based on correct principles becomes a personal constitution, the basis for making major, life-directing decisions, the basis for making daily decisions in the midst of the circumstances and emotions that affect our lives. It empowers individuals with timeless strength in the midst of change.

p.108

November 5

DEVELOPING A WIN/WIN performance agreement* is the central activity of management. Employees can manage themselves within the framework of that agreement, and the manager then can serve like a pace car in a race. He can get things going and then get out of the way. His job from then on is to remove the oil spills.

p.227

* For free examples of win-win agreements and a sample form to create your own, please call 1-800-292-6839.

EFFICIENT MANAGEMENT WITHOUT effective leadership is, as one individual has phrased it, "like straightening deck chairs on the *Titanic*."

p.102

BECAUSE YOU AREN'T omniscient, you can't always know in advance what is truly important. As carefully as you organize the week, there will be times when, as a principle-centered person, you will need to subordinate your schedule to a higher value. Because you are principle-centered, you can do that with an inner sense of peace.

p.169

WHEN WE MAKE deposits of unconditional love, when we live the primary laws of love, we encourage others to live the primary laws of life. In other words, when we truly love others without condition, without strings, we help them feel secure and safe and validated and affirmed in their essential worth, identity, and integrity. Their natural growth process is encouraged. We make it easier for them to live the laws of life—cooperation, contribution, self-discipline, integrity—and to discover and live true to the highest and best within them.

p.199

A CHARACTER RICH in integrity, maturity, and Abundance Mentality has a genuineness that goes far beyond technique, or lack of it, in human interaction.

p.220

FROM RELATIONSHIPS FLOW the agreements that give definition and direction to Win/Win. They are sometimes called *performance agreements* or *partnership agreements*, shifting the paradigm of productive interaction from vertical to horizontal, from hovering supervision to self-supervision, from positioning to being partners in success.

p.223

IF I REALLY want to improve my situation, I can work on the one thing over which I have control—myself. I can stop trying to shape up my wife and work on my own weaknesses. I can focus on being a great marriage partner, a source of unconditional love and support. Hopefully, my wife will feel the power of proactive example and respond in kind. But whether she does or doesn't, the most positive way I can influence my situation is to work on myself, on my *being*.

p.90

PROBABLY THE GREATEST benefit you will experience from exercising will be the development of your muscles of proactivity. As you act based on the value of physical well-being, instead of reacting to all the forces that keep you from exercising, your paradigm of yourself, your self-esteem, your self-confidence, and your integrity will be profoundly affected.

p.292

IN CHOOSING OUR response to circumstance, we powerfully affect our circumstance. When we change one part of the chemical formula, we change the nature of the results.

p.86

TAKING INITIATIVE DOES not mean being pushy, obnoxious, or aggressive. It does mean recognizing our responsibility to make things happen.

p.75

EVEN IN THE midst of people or circumstances that seem to ignore the principles, we can be secure in the knowledge that principles are bigger than people or circumstances, and that thousands of years of history have seen them triumph, time and time again. Even more important, we can be secure in the knowledge that we can validate them in our own lives, by our own experience.

p.122–23

BY CENTERING OUR lives on correct principles, we create a solid foundation for development of the four life-support factors.

Our *security* comes from knowing that, unlike other centers based on people or things that are subject to frequent and immediate change, correct principles do not change.

Our *wisdom* and *guidance* come from correct maps, from the way things really are, have been, and will be.

Our personal *power* is that of a self-aware, knowledgeable, proactive individual, unrestricted by the attitudes, behaviors, and actions of others or by many of the circumstances and environmental influences that limit other people.

p.122–23

As YOU WORK to develop a paradigm that empowers you to see through the lens of importance rather than urgency, you will increase your ability to organize and execute every week of your life around your deepest priorities, to walk your talk. You will not be dependent on any other person or thing for the effective management of your life.

p.179

As YOU LEARN to listen deeply to other people, you will discover tremendous differences in perception. You will also begin to appreciate the impact that these differences can have as people try to work together in interdependent situations.

p.253

DON'T PUSH; BE patient; be respectful. People don't have to open up verbally before you can empathize. You can empathize all the time with their behavior. You can be discerning, sensitive, and aware and you can live outside your autobiography when that is needed.

p.258

I'VE COME TO believe that the key to interpersonal synergy is intrapersonal synergy, that is, synergy within ourselves. The heart of intrapersonal synergy gives the internal security sufficient to handle the risks of being open and vulnerable. By internalizing our principles, we develop authenticity and the abundance mentality of Win/Win.

p.274–75

ANYTIME WE THINK the problem is "out there," that thought is the problem. We empower what's out there to control us. The change paradigm is "outside-in"—what's out there has to change before we can change.

The proactive approach is to change from the inside-out: to *be* different, and by being different, to effect positive change in what's out there—I can *be* more resourceful, I can *be* more diligent, I can *be* more creative, I can *be* more cooperative.

p.89

As WE EXAMINE our scripting carefully, many of us will also begin to see beautiful scripts, positive scripts that have been passed down to us, which we have blindly taken for granted. Real self-awareness helps us to appreciate those scripts and to appreciate those who have gone before us and nurtured us in principle-based living, mirroring back to us not only what we are, but what we can become.

p.315

GIVING A POSITIVE reflection to others in no way diminishes us. It increases us because it increases the opportunities for effective interaction with other proactive people.

p.300

SOMETIMES THE MOST proactive thing we can do is to *be* happy, just to genuinely smile. Happiness, like unhappiness, is a proactive choice.

p.90

PARADIGMS ARE INSEPARABLE from character. *Being* is *seeing* in the human dimension. And what we *see* is highly interrelated to what we *are*. We can't go very far to change our seeing without simultaneously changing our being, and vice versa.

p.32

OUR RESPONSE TO any mistake affects the quality of the next moment. It is important to immediately admit and correct our mistakes so that they have no power over that next moment and we are empowered again.

p.91

CERTAINLY YOU CAN pick up that room better than a child, but the key is that you want to empower the child to do it. You have to get involved in the training and development. It takes time, but how valuable that time is downstream! It saves you so much in the long run.

p.178

REBELLION IS A knot of the heart, not of the mind. The key is to make deposits—constant deposits of unconditional love.

p.199

November 29

THE TRADITIONAL EVALUATION games people play are awkward and emotionally exhausting. In Win/Win, people evaluate themselves, using the criteria that they themselves helped to create up front. And if you set it up correctly, people can do that. With a Win/Win delegation agreement, even a seven-year-old boy can tell for himself how well he's keeping the yard "green and clean."

p.227

GOETHE TAUGHT, "TREAT a man as he is and he will remain as he is. Treat a man as he can and should be and he will become as he can and should be."

p.301

You can value the difference in other people. When someone disagrees with you, you can say, "Good! You see it differently." You don't have to agree with them; you can simply affirm them. And you can seek to understand.

p.284

AS PROACTIVE PEOPLE, we can carry our own physical or social weather with us. We can be happy and accept those things that at present we can't control, while we focus our efforts on the things that we can.

p.90

OUR BASIC NATURE is to act, and not be acted upon. As well as enabling us to choose our response to particular circumstances, this empowers us to create circumstances.

p.75

THE MORE PROACTIVE you are (Habit 1), the more effectively you can exercise personal leadership (Habit 2) and management (Habit 3) in your life. The more effectively you manage your life (Habit 3), the more renewing activities you can do (Habit 7). The more you seek first to understand (Habit 5), the more effectively you can go for synergetic Win/Win solutions (Habits 4 and 6). The more you improve in any of the habits that lead to independence (Habits 1, 2, and 3), the more effective you will be in interdependent situations (Habits 4, 5, and 6). And renewal (Habit 7) is the process of renewing all the habits.

p.303

HABIT 7 "SHARPEN the Saw" is personal Production Capability. It's preserving and enhancing the greatest asset you have—you. It's renewing the four dimensions of your nature—physical, spiritual, mental and social/emotional.

p.288

RENEWAL IS THE principle—and the process—
that empowers us to move on an upward spiral
of growth and change, of continuous improvement.

p.304

OUR BEHAVIOR IS governed by principles. Living in harmony with them brings positive consequences; violating them brings negative consequences. We are free to choose our response in any situation, but in doing so, we choose the attendant consequence. "When we pick up one end of the stick, we pick up the other."

p.90–91

December 8

As we sincerely seek to understand and integrate deep principles into our lives, I am convinced we will discover and rediscover the truth of T.S. Eliot's observation:

We must not cease from exploration and the end of all our exploring will be to arrive where we began and to know the place for the first time.

p.44

WIN/WIN IS NOT a personality technique. It's a total paradigm of human interaction. It comes from a character of integrity, maturity, and the Abundance Mentality. It grows out of high-trust relationships. It is embodied in agreements that effectively clarify and manage expectations as well as accomplishment. It thrives in supportive systems. And it is achieved through empathic communication and synergy.

p.233–34

EMPATHIC LISTENING TAKES time, but it doesn't take anywhere near as much time as it takes to back up and correct misunderstandings when you're already miles down the road, to redo, to live with unexpressed and unsolved problems, to deal with the results of not giving people psychological air.

p.253

THE MORE DEEPLY you understand other people, the more you will appreciate them, the more reverent you will feel about them. To touch the soul of another human being is to walk on holy ground.

p.258

THE SPIRITUAL DIMENSION is your core, your center, your commitment to your value system. It's a very private area of life and a supremely important one. It draws upon the sources that inspire and uplift you and tie you to the timeless truths of all humanity. And people do it very, very differently.

p.292

TRUST IS THE highest form of human motivation. It brings out the very best in people. But it takes time and patience, and it doesn't preclude the necessity to train and develop people so that their competency can rise to the level of that trust.

p.178

THE SINGLE MOST powerful investment we can ever make in life is investment in ourselves, in the only instrument we have with which to deal with life and to contribute. We are the instruments of our own performance, and to be effective, we need to recognize the importance of taking time regularly to sharpen the saw.

p.289

YOUR PARADIGM IS the source from which your attitudes and behaviors flow. A paradigm is like a pair of glasses; it affects the way you see everything in your life. If you look at things through the paradigm of correct principles, what you see in life is dramatically different from what you see through any other centered paradigm.

p.125

WE ARE RESPONSIBLE for our own effectiveness, for our own happiness, and ultimately, I would say, for most of our circumstances.

p.93

THERE ARE SOME people who interpret "proactive" to mean pushy, aggressive, or insensitive; but that isn't the case at all. Proactive people aren't pushy. They're smart, they're value driven, they read reality, and they know what's needed.

p.88

TEST THE PRINCIPLE of proactivity for thirty days and see what happens. Make small commitments and keep them. Be a light, not a judge. Be a model, not a critic. Be part of the solution, not part of the problem.

p.92–93

December 19

IF OUR EMOTIONAL Bank Account is high, credibility is no longer an issue. We're focused on the issues, not on personalities or positions. Because we trust each other, we're open. We put our cards on the table. We're both committed to try to understand each other's point of view deeply and to work together for the Third Alternative, the synergistic solution, that will be a better answer for both of us.

p.221

SEEKING THE THIRD alternative is a major paradigm shift from the dichotomous, either/or mentality. But look at the differences in results!

p.274

INSECURE PEOPLE THINK that all reality should be amenable to their paradigms. They have a high need to clone others, to mold them over into their own thinking. They don't realize that the very strength of the relationship is in having another point of view. Sameness is uncreative . . . and boring. The essence of synergy is to value the differences.

p.274

December 22

WHEN WE MAKE withdrawals from the Emotional Bank Account, we need to apologize and we need to do it sincerely. Great deposits come in the sincere words:

"I was wrong."

"That was unkind of me."

"I showed you no respect,"

"I gave you no dignity, and I'm deeply sorry."

p.197

SEEKING TO UNDERSTAND requires consideration; seeking to be understood takes courage. Win/Win requires a high degree of both.

p.255

RENEWING OUR SOCIAL/EMOTIONAL dimension does not take time in the same sense that renewing the other dimensions does. We can do it in our normal everyday interactions with other people. But it definitely requires exercise. We may have to push ourselves because many of us have not achieved the level of Private Victory and the skills of Public Victory necessary.

p.297

BALANCED RENEWAL IS optimally synergetic. The things you do to sharpen the saw in any one dimension have positive impact in other dimensions because they are so highly interrelated. Your physical health affects your mental health; your spiritual strength affects your social/emotional strength. As you improve in one dimension, you increase your ability in other dimensions as well.

p.303

To MAKE MEANINGFUL and consistent progress along the spiral of growth and improvement, we need to consider *conscience*—the endowment that senses our congruence or disparity with correct principles and lifts us toward them—when it's in shape.

Just as the education of nerve and sinew is vital to the excellent athlete and education of the mind is vital to the scholar, education of the conscience is vital to the truly proactive, highly effective person. Training and educating the conscience, however, requires even greater concentration, more balanced discipline, more consistently honest living. It requires regular feasting on inspiring literature, thinking noble thoughts and, above all, living in harmony with its still, small voice.

p.305

THE PROACTIVE APPROACH to a mistake is to acknowledge it instantly, correct and learn from it. This literally turns a failure into a success. "Success," said IBM founder T. J. Watson, "is on the far side of failure."

p.91

INTRINSIC SECURITY DOESN'T come from what other people think of us or how they treat us. It doesn't come from our circumstances or our position.

It comes from within. It comes from accurate paradigms and correct principles deep in our own mind and heart. It comes from inside-out congruence, from living a life of integrity in which our daily habits reflect our deepest values.

p.298

SOMEONE ONCE INQUIRED of a Far Eastern Zen master, who had a great serenity and peace about him no matter what pressures he faced, "How do you maintain that serenity and peace?" He replied, "I never leave my place of meditation." He meditated early in the morning and for the rest of the day, he carried the peace of those moments with him in his mind and heart.

p.294

IT IS SAID that wars are won in the general's tent. Sharpening the saw in the first three dimensions—the physical, the spiritual, and the mental—is a practice I call the "Daily Private Victory." And I commend to you the simple practice of spending one hour a day every day doing it—one hour a day for the rest of your life.

There's no other way you could spend an hour that would begin to compare in terms of value and results. It will affect every decision, every relationship. It will greatly improve the quality, the effectiveness, of every other hour of the day, including the depth and restfulness of your sleep. It will build the long-term physical, spiritual, and mental strength to enable you to handle difficult challenges in life.

p.296

I BELIEVE THAT as human beings, we cannot perfect ourselves. To the degree to which we align ourselves with correct principles, divine endowments will be released within our nature in enabling us to fulfill the measure of our creation. In the words of Teilhard de Chardin, "We are not human beings having a spiritual experience. We are spiritual beings having a human experience."

p.319

Learn the 7 Habits of Highly Effective People:

Habit 1—Be Proactive: The habit of being proactive, or the habit of personal vision, means taking responsibility for our attitudes and actions. Take the initiative and the responsibility to make things happen.

Habit 2—Begin with the End in Mind: This is the habit of personal leadership. Start with a clear destination to understand where you are now, where you're going, and what you value most.

Habit 3—Put First Things First: This is the habit of personal management, which involves organizing and managing time and events. Manage yourself. Organize and execute around priorities.

Habit 4—Think Win-Win: Win-Win is the habit of interpersonal leadership. Win-Win is the attitude of seeking mutual benefit. This thinking begins with a commitment to explore all options until a mutually satisfactory solution is reached, or to make no deal at all.

Habit 5—Seek First to Understand, Then to Be Understood: This is the habit of empathic communication. Understanding builds the skills of empathic listening that inspire openness and trust.

Habit 6—Synergize: This is the habit of creative cooperation or teamwork. Synergy results from valuing differences by bringing different perspectives together in the spirit of mutual respect.

Habit 7—Sharpen the Saw: This is the habit of self-renewal. Preserving and enhancing your greatest asset, yourself, by renewing the physical, spiritual, mental, and social/emotional dimensions of your nature.

About the Author

Stephen R. Covey is chairman of the Covey Leadership Center and the nonprofit Institute for Principle-Centered Leadership. His firm teaches personal and organizational leadership development worldwide. He has a Harvard MBA and a doctorate from Brigham Young University where he is an adjunct professor at the Marriott School of Management. He is sought after internationally as a speaker and author on leadership, personal effectiveness and change, family, and interpersonal relationships. He is married to Sandra Merrill Covey; they have nine children.

About the Covey Leadership Center

Stephen R. Covey is an internationally respected authority and is founder of the Covey Leadership Center. He has a Harvard MBA and doctorate from Brigham Young University. Author of *The 7 Habits of Highly Effective People* and *Principle-Centered Leadership*. The Covey Leadership Center is a 500-plus member international firm committed to empowering people and organizations to significantly increase their performance capability by applying Principle-Centered Leadership to worthwhile purposes.

The Covey Leadership Center's client portfolio includes 200 of the *Fortune* 500 companies as well as thousands of small and midsize companies, educational institutions, government, and other organizations worldwide. Their work in Principle-Centered Leadership is considered by their clients to be an instrumental foundation to the effectiveness of quality, leadership, service, team building, organizational alignment, and many other strategic corporate initiatives.

Their unique contextual approach to building high-trust cultures by addressing all four levels—personal, interpersonal, managerial, and organizational—is well renowned.

The firm empowers people and organizations to teach themselves and to become independent to the Center. To the adage that goes: "Give a man a fish, you feed him for a day; teach him how to fish and you feed him for a lifetime," is added: "Develop teachers of fishermen and you lift all society." This empowerment process is carried out through programs conducted at the Covey Leadership Center in the Rocky Mountains of Utah, custom corporate on-site programs and consulting, and public 7 Habits and First Things First Time Management seminars offered in over 75 cities in North America and over 40 countries worldwide.

CLC products and programs provide a wide range of resources for individuals, families, business, government, nonprofit, and educational organizations, including:

Programs

Principle-Centered Leadership
  Week
Principle-Centered Leadership &
  Quality
The 7 Habits Internally Facilitated
  Leadership Course
Principle-Centered Leadership
  Internally Facilitated Course
First Things First Time
  Management Course
7 Habits Sales Course
7 Habits Seminars
Seven Habits Renewal Course
Principle-Centered Power Course
7 Habits Family Course
Train the Trainer Courses for
  in-House Certification

Publications

Executive Excellence Newsletter
7 Habits Magazine
7 Habits of Highly Effective People
  Book
Principle-Centered Leadership Book

Products

7 Habits Executive Organizer
7 Habits Audio Tapes
Living the 7 Habits Audio
  Tapes
Principle-Centered Leadership
  Tapes
7 Habits Effectiveness Profile
360 Degree Stakeholder
  Information System
  (organizational diagnosis)
Principle-Centered Living
  Video

Custom Consulting

Custom Principle-Centered
  Leadership Programs
Custom On-Site Programs,
  Consulting, and Speeches
Custom Education Programs

Covey Leadership Center
3507 N. University Avenue
Suite 100
Provo, UT 84604
1-800-292-6839
International: 001-1-801-377-1888
Fax: (801) 342-6236

Please send me:

Registration and pricing information on the Seven Habits course in:

City Name_____

☐ A free Seven Habits application workbook. Contains samples, weekly worksheets, mission statements, self Profile, and win-win agreements.

☐ Information about First Things First/Quadrant II Time Management Courses.

☐ Information about presenters for in-house speeches and keynote addresses.

☐ Information about the in-house video-facilitated course, the Seven Habits of Highly Effective People® for our company.

☐ A free sample of *Executive Excellence* magazine (contributing authors include Stephen R. Covey, Ken Blanchard, Charles Garfield and Warren Bennis).

☐ Information about the Seven Habits of Highly Effective People® audio programs.

Information about Covey Leadership Center® programs and courses on:

☐ Education   ☐ Sales   ☐ Quality   ☐ Leadership   ☐ Family

Demographic Information on Your Company and You:

Number of employees: ☐ under 3,000   ☐ 3,001–10,000
☐ 10,001 +

Income: ☐ $0–$35,000   ☐ $35,001–$75,000   ☐ $75,001 +

(Please do not send this coupon if you have already called.)